FATHER
TO THE MAN

Also by Christopher Hallowell

PEOPLE OF THE BAYOU

GROWING OLD, STAYING YOUNG

FATHER
TO THE MAN

A Journal

CHRISTOPHER
HALLOWELL

William Morrow and Company, Inc. | New York

A portion of this book was previously published in *Glamour*.

Copyright © 1987 by Christopher Hallowell

Library of Congress Cataloging-in-Publication Data

Hallowell, Christopher.
   Father to the man.
   1. Father and child—United States. 2. Fathers and sons—United States. I. Title.
HQ756.H33   1987   306.8′742   86-18013
ISBN 0-688-06516-3

Printed in the United States of America

First Edition

1 2 3 4 5 6 7 8 9 10
BOOK DESIGN BY VICTORIA HARTMAN

The childhood shows the man,
As morning shows the day.

—*John Milton*

Introduction

Matthew never asks why the sky is blue, but he has wondered where the sun goes at night. It does not go anywhere, I have told him; it is the world that is moving, right around the sun. "You mean the world is floating?" he asks incredulously. "But what holds us up?" I do not know the answer. At four and a half, questions pour from him. I can see his mind grow. I love to watch him figure out how things work, to watch his hands explore and to see the intensity of his concentration. Discovery makes him smile and crinkles his eyes with delight.

Maggie, almost two and a half, struts about with a proud waddle that marks the beginning of independence. But she has not yet reached the age of abstract thinking. She is just learning the basics of life. As we walk along a street, she points out to me with an exclamatory finger all she knows: "Dere's a car; dere's a tree; dere's a man; dere's a . . . what's dat?"

To a shocking extent, she fills the sexual stereotype of femininity. She likes to make people feel at ease and laugh. She often does so by dancing for them. "Look, I dancing," she proclaims as she flounders across a floor. She is fastidious. A slight smudge on her hands elicits the alarmed exclamation and command, "Look, I all dirty. Napkin, please. I need napkin." My wife, Willa, and I are concerned about this need for cleanliness. We think that it might have something to do with her being a city kid. A dose of country life might do her some good.

I am fortunate to be in a profession that allows me to work at home. I see my children more than many fathers do. No out of the door at eight in the morning and back in the evening to play with the kids for half an hour before their bedtime. I am informally on call much of the day. My children know where to find me, most often in my office upstairs in our house in New York, hunched over a typewriter and with a bleary look on my face. Matthew is not sure what I do but constantly assures me that I am a good writer. I need that encouragement. Last year he dictated a story to his nursery school teacher. I have it on the wall of my office. "Writers write," it reads. "I want to be a writer because it's a good job. My dad earns money writing. I think I want to do the same work as my dad."

Willa and I have made an effort to share parenting equally. She is a professional photographer who, like me, works out of our home. She is available to the children as much as I. Together, we try to complement each other in our parental duties. Among many couples, it is the mother who often has a full-time job, who is expected to be *the* responsible parent. In doing so, she becomes the family boss as well as its nurturer, an inequitable role that asks too much and leaves the husband/father too little. These men wear bewildered expressions. They have to ask where the baby powder and diapers are kept. They fumble while dressing their children. They lose interest.

The parenting that Willa and I have chosen creates its hardships. There are no traditional roles to rely upon for guidance and security. Conflict and inefficiency hover about, adding one more frustration to already pressured lives. We ask each other whose turn it is to bathe the children, put them to bed, take them to the park. Inevitably, we both perform these duties at the same time. If one of us is busy, trade-offs have to be made and resentments accumulate. I sometimes wish that Willa were a traditional mother who would unquestioningly take care of all the whines and the wiping of runny noses. But then I think of fathers ignorant of the job of seeing sobs transformed into mirth and knowing that they were influential in changing a child's mood from dark and sad to hopeful.

Through my more or less constant presence around the children, I think that I am able to sense many of their needs. But compared to Willa, I am a rank amateur. With the flick of her eye, she can tell that something is bothering one of them. She can sense that they are getting sick even before they feel sick. Yet I am proud that Matthew and Maggie love the way I attend to them, and I assume that it is because I am providing them with a warmth more common to mothers.

I even tell myself that I do not mind getting out of bed at three in the morning to ward off a sleep-induced monster that is about to carry one of them away. "Daddy, Daddy," one of them yells. "Come 'ere. Quick." Both Willa and I are instantly awake and half out of bed, a response ingrained in us from the first night that Matthew came home from the hospital. Invariably, Willa offers to go to their assistance, but we both know what will happen if she does. She will arrive in the crying child's room and be met with screams of "No, I want Daddy, Daddy." So I go to them in the small hours. I take them to the bathroom to pee and tuck them in and tell them that all the monsters or bad guys or mosquitoes or whatever are asleep.

While Willa may appear to be a background parent through the following pages, she is anything but that. Her role as a parent is every bit as active as mine. The difference is that mother-child relationships are more explored while those between fathers and children are full of as-yet-unknown possibilities.

Fathers are curious people, aloof and mysterious, popping in and out of young lives, often having in common a reputation for being distant and preoccupied with their own affairs. A few years ago, I wrote an article touching upon my father's relationship with me that was published in *The New York Times Magazine*. I mentioned my father's hardness and lack of communication. For several weeks after the piece appeared, I received calls and letters from many men who sadly told me that my father and *their* father sounded like the same person.

I also discovered that writing about a member of one's family carries dangers. There is the danger, for one, of being too honest or, from another viewpoint, too biased. After reading the article, some people came to me and said that the man I had described as my father did not sound like the man that they had known. There was the implication that I had been unfair, a charge that has disturbed me. Obviously, those people had not been a son to my father. They had met only his social side, which was far more outgoing and giving than the one he presented to me.

What disturbed me most was the suggestion that I had no right to expose the relationship between a father and son, that weak chinks in a family's structure should be concealed rather than mentioned. I agree in principle. There is a sacredness about the family that should not be violated, but if sons had felt obliged not to write about their fathers, literature would be far less rich than it is. In any case, the relationship that I had with my father is not unique. The tension-fraught unfolding of the father-son relationship rolls on through the generations, producing bewilderment and repetition and the silent wish that fathers be more compassionate. What follows perhaps will be an inspiration. At least it will show that a different side of fatherhood is possible.

During a recent summer, I was able to rearrange various writing commitments so that I could take an entire month off. I wanted the time just to be with my children. I did not want to be with them just anywhere, though. I wanted to go to a special place that I have known since I was a boy younger than Matthew, a place that my father and his father and his father knew. The few families who reside during summers on this insignificant promontory jutting into the Atlantic cherish it for the fact that the world at large might as well not exist. For a few months of the year, it is paradise to them, particularly to their children; a mystery to others who are less aware of its social expectations and mannerisms; and a burden, yet to others. It used to be a burden to me. As a boy, I spent two or three weeks there every summer. It is difficult for a child to dislike a secluded seaside retreat that offers complete physical freedom, but I came close to it. My family never indoctrinated me into its social niceties or prepared me for the pressures that are an understood part of this place's traditions. I was timid, socially inept, physically awkward, and at times, I fear, considered a loss by the family.

Children should not respond to paradise so sadly. It took me years to understand the uniqueness of this little peninsula. I had to cast off family, learn to laugh at their sometimes ludicrous expectations; I had to accept that my father, the most influential person in my life, was a self-centered man so insecure in his sense of self that he insisted that I be molded in his image as a form of self-justification. Even now, well on the far side of youth, I feel the remnants of fears acquired during childhood clamp down on my adult brain when I am in this community. They partially paralyze my ability to think and to respond. But I have learned to love the place for other reasons.

I never want my children to have to learn that love. I want them to just love this rare gathering of people, water, boats, and fragrant pines for what they are by passing days there unconscious of any other time and place.

FATHER
TO THE MAN

August 3

The children are in a frenzy of fatigue and boredom. Howls of anguish and grating whines extinguish any attempt at civilized conversation. The car smells of peanut butter and rotten bananas. Story books, coloring books, tape cassettes, and stuffed animals litter the floor and seats. People passing us on the highway stare up at the roof and smile. They see a mountain of paraphernalia that immediately marks us as another American family beginning its summer vacation.

For the duration of the six hours that the trip has taken from New York, beset with traffic tie-ups and pee- and hamburger-stops, Matthew has asked how long it would be before we arrive. The questioning began somewhere in the Bronx, and there I began the countdown.

"Four hundred and twenty minutes," I answered. The sound of minutes offers so many more possibilities for the rapid passage of time than hours. Every ten minutes or so, he has repeated the question, and each time I have subtracted ten minutes, to which he has replied, "Oh, we're getting really close now."

And now, we *are* really close. At New Bedford, the first place where sea gulls float with obvious familiarity above the traffic, Maggie bobs up and down in her child's seat, saying, "We near ocean now. We near ocean. Look, look, see gull. Dere's a gull. I see gull."

Soon we pass landmarks from past visits—the antique shop where Ben, the friendly Labrador retriever, lives; the supermarket so dear to Matthew and Maggie because it has a big bin of animal crackers; the fire station where Maggie comments, "Fi-engine sleeping. Have nice sleep, fi-engine"; the pizza place, and down the road through the marsh, there's Weenaumet Point. The marsh separates the Point from the rest of the world. Fields of grass on each side of us give the road a fragility, as if it were merely tolerated by this soggy stretch of half-water half-land. Sometimes it isn't. A strong wind helped by a full moon and a high tide can push water right over the road, cutting the Point's link to the outside world as effectively as a deep-water channel.

On the other side of the marsh, the road's asphalt narrows slightly, and its sandy shoulders broaden. Scrub oaks and pitch pines block any view of the nearby ocean. The only evidence of human habitation are driveways that disappear into the underbrush and paths that emerge from the woods on one side of the road and pop back in on the other. Bare-footed children can sometimes be seen darting along one of them like Indians. The paths crisscross the neck, beaten generations ago out of the poison ivy and catbrier and blueberry bushes. They link each house to its neighbor, and eventually all lead to the community beach.

"There's the beach," singsongs Matthew as we drive past it. He always singsongs when he is happiest, a kind of melodious contentment. And then down the long straight driveway that leads to the house and the sea. Its unfolding through the soft-smelling pines bring back ten thousand bittersweet memories. I have walked its length countless times ever since I was Maggie's age.

"There's the tennis court," singsongs Matthew. "Daddy, I wan' to play tennis." I have just given him a child's tennis racket. He holds it like a baseball bat and is all set to hit home runs with it. As we drive past, I see a scene out of my childhood, of my father and me on the court, he patiently but without inspiration teaching me the game. I am always scared to tell him how bored I am, scared that he will think less of me than he already seems to.

The driveway divides, and we take the right fork, a newer cut through the undergrowth. It leads to a modest, suburban-looking house with a wide deck overlooking the sea and a roof so slightly pitched as to give the structure a squashed appearance. It is partially mine now, shared with my sister and her family, an inheritance that we can scarcely comprehend our good fortune to have received. The house's interior is of knotty pine—knotty pine everywhere—bedroom walls, kitchen walls, hall walls. It used to bring to mind scenes of hunting cabins in cheap movies climaxed by horrible bloody violence. But now I find the walls more tolerable. The knots have lost their sinister gleam. The wood smells of salt and sun and reminds me of summer days in shorts and bare feet.

It is past the children's bedtime when we arrive, and we put them straight to bed, or we try to. Matthew presents little problem after the usual half hour's procrastination during which I am persuaded to push him on the deck swing, pour him a glass of apple juice, run with him down the worn path that leads to the rocky beach so we can look at the water (and taste it to make sure it is salty), and pay a visit to the raccoon-ravaged garden to see if there are any surviving cornstalks. We climb into bed, and

I read him *Scuppers, The Sailor Dog,* a book that is sure to put the sea into his dreams. He is asleep within two minutes of our finishing it.

Maggie is not so easy. Nightfall brings the wind moaning. Even with windows and doors closed, it finds a crack. The sound is one of the most calming that I know, and I always try to increase its volume and pitch by opening the windows wide. Maggie is not lulled by it one bit. It reminds her of thunder. Three weeks earlier a nighttime thunderstorm burst over New York, terrifying her. We sat her in our bed and read her a dozen books. After we finished, she was still wide awake and ran through her growing repertoire of reasons that she could not go to sleep. She was hungry, she was thirsty, she had to go doo-doo, etcetera. Now she thinks any strange sound she hears when she is in bed is thunder. Alarm grows in her coal-black eyes as she becomes conscious of the wind's blowing. "Dat t'under?" she asks. She is not convinced when I tell her that it is only the wind.

"I no go to bed. I get up." With the determination that a two-and-a-half-year-old can muster with surprising ease, she begins crawling out of the covers. "I go out."

"No, Maggie," I say. "Everyone's going to bed now. You too." Her resolve softens, and she allows me to put her back in bed.

"No close door. You leave light on," she orders.

"Sure, Maggie," I reply with a hint of sarcasm playing in my voice.

"Daddy, what's dat noise?" An especially loud moan has come through her closed window. The bedroom is hot, and the air is still.

"That's the wind talking. That's one of Daddy's favorite sounds."

"You like dat sound," she chirps.

"Yes, it makes me go to sleep," and I yawn for emphasis.

"Oh, I go sleep. You leave light on. You no close door."

All is quiet save for the wind's comforting moaning and the soft sounds of Willa unpacking suitcases. I wander into the living room and turn to the fireplace mantel, an unconscious movement that I catch myself doing each time I come to the house after a long absence. I turn toward my father, the most dominant force in my life when I was a boy and still influential though dead for seven years. He stares at me from two fading photographs. I stare back, hoping to discover some chink in his expression that I have not noticed before, a suggestion in the deep-set eyes of why he held such power and so blithely abused it. I see nothing new. The way he is in the photographs is how I remember him so often. In one, he is racing the family sailboat, beating to windward, swells and whitecaps surrounding the little hull. His head is slightly inclined, and he is peering ahead with the intensity of a pointer staring down a bird. I know the pose. He is judging whether he can make the racing buoy on this tack or whether he will have to waste precious seconds by coming around and going off on the other. He is total concentration and murmured monologue. "The tide is helping us, but we're getting into a chop. Now dammit, look at that boat over there. She's going like hell. Well, I don't know. If we stay here, we'll have to pinch her and lose too much. If we tack, we might just get an extra breeze. Hell, we'll tack. Ready about. Hardalee." Whether he tacks or not, he is constantly sailing right through the house's living room.

I could be in the boat with him, and was many times, huddled against the mast, soaked and shivering, thinking that this kind of racing must be the slowest sport known to man. But for him the weekend races were the meat of his upbringing. Winning the race brought a delusion of total acceptance.

In the other photograph, he is standing in the cockpit of a cruising boat. My mother took the picture; they were sailing with some friends of my father and had just come into a harbor for the night. He is wearing a grin that most people find charming. I know differently. He has just finished saying something sarcastic to my mother—perhaps about her persistent inability to operate a camera properly—and now he is waiting for her reaction of mock outrage. Behind the grin, he is angry. My mother hated sailing and feared boats, a fear that she could never overcome and that my father never understood.

Photographs of handsome old schooners that sailed out of my father's past decorate the walls of every room. Open a closet door and there hangs a suit of sails from one boat or another. The basement is full of salvaged gear—blocks and lines and stays and shackles—scrounged from minor wrecks delivered to the rocks in front of the house.

Dead these eight years, and the house is still in his name as is the post office box and the telephone listing. I wonder why I keep the photographs of him on the mantel. For several years after his death, I turned them down whenever I came to the house and felt guilty for doing so. But his face would not go away. Now I just leave them there and happily realize that the pain he caused is gradually diminishing each year. I wonder how I will feel at the end of the month. Perhaps his constant presence during the time will enable me to come to terms with him. But it would be impossible to rid the house of my father. You can sweep the cobwebs from a seaside house everyday, but the spiders remain.

Maggie sleeps until five o'clock, when a blue jay outside her window lets out a shriek. She startles awake with a wail: "Daddy, com'ere. I hear t'under. You come here!"

I drag myself out of bed and tell her that a bird made the noise and recite to her the names of everyone she knows and that they are asleep, a trick that usually works. "Matthew asleep, Mommy asleep, Grandma asleep, Grandpa asleep, Margo asleep, Rob asleep. . . ." It takes. She sticks her thumb in her mouth and closes her eyes.

The peace lasts for an hour until a training jet from a nearby air force base breaks the sound barrier with a blast that really does sound like thunder.

She awakens again, and this time it is too hard to explain to her what made the sound. I get into bed with her and read her a favorite story about a little boy with a drum who got up early one morning and, playing his drum, led a procession of animals out of sight over the top of a hill. He does a lot of "rum-a-tum-tumming" on the way. At each one, Maggie looks up at me and asks, "Boy make t'under?"

August 4

"Where do you want to sail to?" I ask Matthew. We are in *Song Sparrow*, the family's Herreschoff twelve-and-a-half-footer, one of a beamy, gaff-rigged class with stubby mast that used to plow through and bob over Buzzards Bay's swells in fleets. Now restricted to only a few harbors, they are treated with enormous affection, like family dogs that all the children have grown up with. From a distance, they look ridiculously small on the water.

"Let's go to Africa, Dad." We often imagine taking trips, sometimes to distant planets, sometimes no farther than a foreign city. Matthew prances about the boat like a sprite, feeling every inch of her against his body. He lies down on the leeward floorboards and peers into the sloshing bilge. He inches up on the little foredeck and, belly flattened against the canvas, hangs his head over to windward, the spray wetting his cheeks. A wave slaps the gunwale and drenches him. He laughs. "Dad, did you see that? How did that happen?"

"Maybe it was a whale waving with his tail," I say.

"No, I think it was that last dinosaur. Maybe a lobster just pinched him and he jumped." Matthew's curiosity about dinosaurs suddenly diminished one day when he came back from a trip to the American Museum of Natural History and informed us that "all the dinosaurs died a long, long time ago, even before you were born, Daddy." Still, the possibility lurks in his mind that there may be a few dinosaurs left, a possibility that I encourage.

It occurs to me that Matthew could fall overboard with all his jumping about, but I am not too worried about it. The Styrofoam bubble strapped to his back would keep him afloat. Besides, I am watching carefully where he steps and I am impressed by his care and his surefootedness. He has always been cautious beyond his age, never jumping unless he knows exactly what he is going to land on. Maggie is quite the opposite. Ask her to put her hand in a dark hole, and she'll look up with trust in her eyes and say, "Okay. What's dere, candy?" Matthew will lean down and look into the hole first and then believe a monster waits within. I wonder if the difference is genetic. We worried about Matthew's caution for a time, especially when he hung back in a playground, afraid to climb the jungle gym or go down the slide. Now we rejoice in his caution and worry about Maggie's lack of concern, our attitudes flip-flopping like a fish washed upon a beach.

"Ready about. Hardalee," I yell. The boat comes into the wind, her sails flapping before they fill again and she falls off, heading more or less at right angles to our previous direction. We sail in silence for five minutes or so. The perpetual southwest wind freshens and heels us over more. Matthew leans over the leeward rail and drags his fingers in the water so that it sprays up in rooster tails. I remember doing that to my father's stern warning: "You're slowing the boat. Take your hand out of the water right now." I always wondered why I never felt the boat surge forward when I complied. Matthew's fascination with the play of the water against his hand absorbs me so much that we almost ram a buoy.

We beat out into the bay, heading for Africa. Just off the port bow, we see nothing but water ahead. We are in the open ocean and Africa lies beyond the horizon. The wind whistles between the mainsail and jib, a low, mournful sound that easily lets me imagine that we have been hearing it for months as we finally near the wild coast that we know will be our first sight of Africa. Off to starboard I can see a small schooner's bow plunging in the swell, spray slapping her deck. The maze of lines coming off the bowsprit's point and rising to the foremast give the craft an antiquated look. If I fix my stare at the boat's prow, I can imagine that we are sailing abeam a smuggler or a pirate ship.

"Daddy, are there any pirates here?"

I have not noticed that Matthew has taken his hand out of the water and is staring at the schooner as well. To a child, she could well be a pirate ship, a wicked ship with black combing and heavy ratlines running up her spars and patched umber sails and a cruel captain who throws children to crocodiles.

Neverland is very much alive in Matthew's mind. I had told him that pirates still frequent the waters of some oceans. His mind is filled with images that he can barely control.

"That's a real pirate ship, I think," he states worriedly.

We are closing in on the rock-strewn coast of Weenaumet. "There's Africa," I exclaim.

With a little smile quivering his lips, he stares at the shoreline along which he has walked many times before. He sees our house tucked into the pines, but his eyes quickly pass over it. "Look, Daddy, look. There are some elephants!" he yells.

"Where?" I ask.

"Right behind those rocks, see. There's a mommy and a daddy and two children. And I see an ostrich. He's running. Daddy, did you know that an ostrich can run faster than a lion?"

"Matthew," I shout. "Look in the water. Crocodiles. We'd better tack."

We are getting close to shore; I see rocks lurking beneath the waves. We tack.

"Whew, that was close," I say. "They won't get us now."

Matthew looks into the water, his face clouded with worry. "Dad, did you really see crocodiles? They could bite our heads off, right?"

We veer away from the coast of Africa. I ask Matthew if he wants to sail the boat, and he jumps to the tiller. But he is not really interested in steering. He is more interested in just being on the boat. I explain that if he pulls the tiller toward him, the boat will head off from the wind. But he doesn't care. Seeing him so engrossed in the phenomenon of floating on water and rising over the waves, I don't care either.

We are far out now. The coast of Africa has grown smaller. The lighthouse in the bay is so close that we can see the twinkle of its beacon. It's time to start back toward the harbor. But the tall tower sitting on the bulk of the light's foundation has awakened a dinosaur in Matthew's mind, perhaps the last one. "Dad, look behind you. There's *Tyrannosaurus rex* coming. He's going to get us."

I look astern toward the light and gasp. "Ready about. Hardalee," I shout. *Song Sparrow* plunges off toward safety. "We did it, Matthew," I cry excitedly. "We got away." Matthew is looking at me quizzically. "Dad, there aren't any more dinosaurs, really, are there? That's what I learned at the Museum of Natural History."

Once again, I suggest that somewhere there might be just one more left.

We are going before the wind now on our way back to the harbor. Swells chase the stern and look as if they are going to climb over us before slipping under the hull and pushing us forward in a downward surge of gurgling bubbles. The boat stops dead in the trough before the next swell lifts us up. The sun is beginning to set astern, filling each swell with golden light.

Matthew lies on the stern deck, his chin resting on the transom, his eyes watching the glowing water. They widen in alarm as each swell approaches and relax as it passes underneath the hull.

He breaks the peace of the rhythm and turns to me.

"Dad, where can we sail to tomorrow? I want to go to that country where kangaroos live."

"Okay," I say, "we'll sail to Australia tomorrow."

August 5

Maggie is still too young to feel the freedom that Ween-aumet can offer. Her main preoccupation at the moment is to determine whether she is a person or a dog. Her confusion results from our acquisition of an eleven-week-old mostly German shepherd puppy. Matthew named her Brio, in honor of his adored Swedish-made wooden train set of that name. Over the past few days Maggie has fortunately leaned toward believing that she is a member of the human species. We know this because she comes up to us with a definitive but still questioning look in her eye and announces, "Maggie not Brio, Maggie person." She wants us to affirm this fact, though from her point of view the similarities between her and the puppy may be greater than the differences. They are of the same height. Both are in awe of the world around them. Neither can control bladder or bowel. Both are fascinated by rolling balls and pull toys. But Maggie has discerned some differences, and we expressively agree with her that she is a person.

Matthew's eyes are wide open to the sights and sounds around him, a steady smile playing on his lips. A year earlier, my uncle, watching Matthew gazing at sailboats in the bay observed, "One summer here and it will be in his bones." Maybe he is right; he speaks from life-long attachment. The essence of the Point, from bay-scented breezes to the sound of water lapping at gunwales, seems already to be settling over Matthew to hold him in a gossamer net. He may become a lifetime captive, as has happened to so many, cherishing the grip that holds them. Well over half the adult members of the fifty or so families living on the Point spent their childhood summers among its boats and blueberry bushes.

To members of the older generation, the Point is a quiet religion, and life without its traditions would be a sparser one. More than a summer refuge from the outside world, it is a place to which the outside world bears little relationship. It is not that people here shut themselves off from outsiders—they are a friendly lot in general—but that unarticulated subtleties, the way a person talks or even walks, for example, instantly says if one is part of the tradition or a newcomer with a different history and set of values.

While the older generation assumes that the Point's comfortable seclusion is their birthright, their offspring return to its simplicity only after having rebelled against its seemingly unchanging nature. It is their own children who bring them back, for Weenaumet is above all a place for children. And what parent can not take joy in intro-ducing his or her children to the same experiences that he had during his own childhood. In this way parents, too, return to childhood. They are amazed that what they re-jected so long ago is still intact while all the world about them is changing so jarringly. That continuity can be a rare art form is an awe-inspiring realization, one that brings a person to a fuller awareness each day.

This paradise was born in 1888. Before that Weenau-met was a two-mile-long sheep farm, its only structure a broken wooden tugboat hard on the rocks at its tip. Even in those days, real estate speculators cast about for cheap land. Four proper Bostonians purchased its five hundred acres despite being told by residents of the nearby town that "it wa'n't worth nothin'," as a local history of the region tells it. The investors were experienced real estate people; one had made a fortune buying nearby land cheap and selling it dear; another had done the same north of Boston. Before long, though, they realized that their investment in Weenaumet was a foolish one, but not before one of them had built a massive stone and wood structure for himself. He discovered his mistake as soon as he moved in: Mosquitoes infested the Point. Swarms of them hovered about him and his family like dark clouds. Welts puffed up their exposed skin. He abandoned the place after one summer's residence.

Much later my great-grandfather rented the house during summers. A colonel during the Civil War, he was portrayed eternally on a white horse. Accounts of Civil War campaigns, in which he led a black regiment, consistently mention him on his white horse. A friend of mine, a black man, was named after him. The man's family lived in a town near Philadelphia from which many members of the Colonel's regiment came. After the war ended, the Colonel rode his white horse down the town's main street while giving thanks to his soldiers. Years later, my friend's family gave him my great-grandfather's surname as his first name.

Histories of Harvard University recount the Colonel exercising his white horse in Harvard Yard. And a history of Weenaumet mentions that he rode his white horse back and forth the quarter-mile distance between the big house and the communal beach, stopping along the way to chat with neighbors.

The house still stands, a monolith rising above the scrub pines. It dwarfs the newer dwellings that hide in the underbrush. I have a photograph of my great-grandfather in front of the house when he was older, long after his white horse was retired. He is holding my father, then about Matthew's age, on his knee. Both are looking at the camera. Through the old man's tremendous white mustache and badly trimmed goatee, a quietly mirthful face peers out. My father has a shy look, but his shoulders are square and his chin juts out as if he is terribly proud to be in the embrace of this hero.

Long before the photograph was taken, the investors sold the infested land to another group of speculators, the real founders of Weenaumet as it is today. The group saw the property not so much as a real estate bonanza as a place that could be divided up and parceled out to friends—one of whom was my great-grandfather—and settled down upon for peaceful summers. But first, the mosquitoes had to be dealt with.

Here is what one of the principals wrote about his first visit to the Point in 1903:

> My father proposed that we should all go over from Mattapoisett, where we were then living, to see the new land.... The moment we crossed the causeway the horse turned gray; he was covered with mosquitoes; and my father remarked that before looking at the land we had better drive down to [the end of the Point] where there would be no mosquitoes and we could eat our lunch. We did so, but with a light easterly wind the mosquitoes were nearly as thick there.

In 1903 a great deal of shorefront between Boston and Cape Cod must have been undeveloped. Why these pioneer families persisted with mosquito-ridden Weenaumet is a mystery. But soon "the syndicate," as they humbly called themselves, hired some Italian immigrants to clear the sandy soil of its underbrush so that the southwest wind could free the entire peninsula of insects. Then they had all the low, wet spots, ideal breeding places for mosquitoes, filled in. That took care of half the mosquito population. The other half frequented the marsh that separates the Point from the mainland. Draining the marsh was the solution, one that was not entirely successful, for the marsh still exists, along with its very visible drainage ditches, which channel the inflow and outflow of the tides, thus restricting the mosquitoes. They were no longer a problem. The effort was an ecological success of the nicest kind, getting rid of the insects but keeping the marsh.

The Point's acreage was divided into comfortable "lots" of between four and almost twenty acres. The prospectus advertised the place as being especially accessible to Boston via a train known as the "Dude." The trip took only one hour and twenty minutes, far less time than the train requires today. Those who bought were Boston families, friends of friends to create a harmonious and effortless social network where values and expectations could be shared and conversations comfortably begun, dropped, and taken up again. My father once wrote a vignette of the journey the settlers made each June from Boston and its outskirts to Weenaumet. He remembered this from when he was nine years old; the year would have been 1915:

> First a railroad box car had to be ordered for the siding in West Medford. Then packing cases appeared from the cellar and the attic, into which were placed all the linen, blankets, towels, curtains, and a host of miscellaneous paraphernalia needed for a short summer, also a large trunk for each person. Basic food supplies, barrel of flour, barrels of sugar, coffee, tea, crackers, etc., were delivered to the house.
>
> On the appointed day, Wilhemina, Granny's old

horse, and one other were given a morning bath at the
stable; then with two carriages, several wagon loads of
packing boxes, food boxes, upright piano, and a school
boy hired for the summer, the procession started for
the box car. Two stalls had to be improvised for the
horses, the carriages had to be blocked with 2 × 4's,
the piano had to be secured, and a hammock slung for
the hired boy.

Early in the evening the car was packed up and
made part of the night freight. This arrived the next
morning when the car was shunted onto a siding
equipped with an unloading ramp. The process was
now reversed and with the help of Mr. McAllister's
horse and wagon everything was, in due course, delivered to the house.

The houses that these people put up had to be large;
five or six children in a family was average. A separate
wing for cooks and maids was required. Nothing was
graceful about these structures. Their presence shifted the
appearance of the Point from a low-lying, monotonous
stretch of shore to a string of bulky residences strong
enough to withstand the buffeting southwest wind and an
occasional hurricane and large enough to hold the offspring of generations who would forever preserve the de-
ceptive simplicity of this little finger of land.

The life-styles set down then are to a large degree the
life-styles of today, though the hired help has long since
vanished. Families rise early. By eight the shouts of children drift through the tangles of catbrier and scrub oak
that separate the houses. By nine, the muffled *thwop* of
tennis balls bouncing on the many courts scattered about
the Point competes with the sporadic but rising cry of cicadas in the treetops. By this time, the children, break-
fasted and clothed, take up those activities that engrave
the Point in their hearts. Fort building on the rocks is one.

Every child between the ages of six and ten is compelled to explore the flotsam that continually washes up on the rocky shore as surely as the rising tide that brings it. Prizes of mysterious provenance await them: lengths of rope, plastic buckets, lobster-pot buoys, plastic sheeting, planks, and the occasional grand prize—a rowboat washed from one shore to another by a storm. As a boy, I spent hours hopping from one rock to the next (an activity in itself if you concentrate on not falling into the crevices between the boulders) in search of building materials for my stone-walled forts. Driftwood planks were essential for roofs. Seaweed laid on top served as shingles and as camouflage. Wooden bait boxes were admirable seats. A cable spool was a real find—an instant table.

Children usually make their forts at the beginning of the summer, and they use them constantly for a week or two before abandoning them for other delights. After summer dwellers have migrated to winter homes, these patchwork creations succumb to foul weather of fall and winter. By the following spring, they are hollow ruins awaiting a fresh crop of military architects by the sea.

Exploring is another childhood activity, and what a place the Point is for that, from the network of paths leading off into the underbrush to the so-called secret passages that connect the rooms of the huge houses. No two paths are the same; each traverses a microenvironment. On one a child can imagine himself in a terrifying jungle of snarled vines and coiled snakes; on another, a pine-needle-carpeted walkway leads to an imaginary castle just visible through the trees; and another promises a pungent rain forest of rotting vegetation and possibilities for other-worldly life. Matthew likes to believe that elves inhabit the undergrowth bordering this path. The little area has thus become known to us as the elf forest, and the path leading through it the only means of viewing its dwellers.

Matthew will run along it, staring wildly at the rotting stumps, briar snarls, and mushrooms that pop through the pine-needle floor. "Elves," he cries. "There's one, there's another. There's one with a red hat!" And then he points in all directions. "Elf, elf, elf!"

The secrets of the houses are treated with a bit more caution. The larger and older ones offer any number of little hidden doors that give access to dusty passages under eaves. Open one slowly and watch a child's eyes widen as the light dispels the darkness within. Just beyond the shaft, a child's imagination can make out another door that leads to a forgotten room of dusty carpets, dull suits of armor, and a box full of jewels. It takes a while to sweep such possibilities and terrors away, but afterward, children are free to roam the passages, soon using them as bunkers, mine shafts, monsters' lairs, or secret meeting places known to adults only by the excited whispers issuing from behind the firmly shut little doors.

The communal beach is the Point's focus for children and adults if the tide is high around midmorning. It serves as far more than a beach, though. It is a clearing area where children get to know each other, adults exchange news and gossip, and newcomers are looked over, not by eyeing them surreptitiously but through forthright introductions, the tenor of response being the cue to acceptance or tolerance. The residents of the Point come from a tradition, after all, of being polite to all and accepting of only a few.

We fall into the routine though Matthew's excitement leads him to want to take advantage of all Weenaumet's offerings simultaneously. As the sun warms the morning and the water sloshes in the bay as it does on hot August days, Matthew blurts out that he wants to go sailing, to play tennis, to walk the secret paths, to catch jellyfish, net minnows in the tidal pool, and pick blueberries.

We discuss the options. The blueberries have another week or so to ripen. Sailing is out of the question until the wind rises. The fishing is better in the early morning. We decide to go to the beach. Upon arriving, Matthew heads for the dock, where he knows he can catch jellyfish, the one species of marine life that offers him the challenge of capture and the fascination of ooze all in one.

There he is in his white sailor hat and blue terrycloth after-swimming robe. He is lying on the dock, face and arms hanging over the water as he waits for jellyfish to drift by, the edges of their membranes shining a magical patina in the green water. Carefully, he cups his hands and scoops one out. "Dad," he yells, "I got one. I got one. Want to see?" I look down at the gelatinous blob in his hands. I exclaim at its size and suggest that he make a peanut butter and jelly sandwich with it. He looks up at me and crinkles his big eyes and says, "No, Dad, that would be yucky. You're funny, Dad."

This place is full of unhappy memories that even now make me sad. They pop up at any time and out of unexpected places. I see one now as I watch Matthew. When I was his age, I fished for jellyfish, too, and made my first catch on the very same dock. My grandmother was sitting on the beach and I ran up to her bursting with pride, "Granny, Granny, look what I caught!" She was in conversation with a friend. "Granny, look, look!"

At last she turned to me and saw what was in my hand. "Ugh," she cried. "Get that horrible thing away from me." I was flabbergasted. I remember wondering if she realized the mistake she was making, that I had done a wonderful thing but she did not realize it. My heart sank, and I turned away from her, the jellyfish oozing between my fingers.

August 6

Beachcombing on Weenaumet is a pastime for members of every generation. Foggy days encourage it. Among the huge rocks strewn along the shore between the water and the sandy turf that anchors scruffy vegetation, yellow-slickered figures appear and disappear in the fog, heads bent over the line of seaweed accumulated by high seas. The brown tangled mat often holds treasures worth nothing save the memory of a gray day when what the Point lost in sparkle it gained in mystery. Today is such a day. The southwest wind pushes layers of fog through the pines, leaving their needles glistening. So moisture-laden is the air that I can feel the wetness entering my lungs as I breathe. Sounds come off the water muffled and fickle. A sail flaps, first from here, then from down the shore. Voices like spirits drift through the whiteness.

We listen as we balance on the damp rocks in front of the house, Maggie on my shoulders and Matthew by my side.

"Daddy, that sounds like ghosts," Matthew says, a quaver in his voice.

"Maybe they're the ghosts of pirates who hid treasure here," I suggest.

"No, Daddy, you're just kidding," retorts Matthew, who can be too wise for his age.

"You funny, Daddy," speaks Maggie's voice from above.

"Let's find the treasure," I say and begin to jump from one big rock to another. At every landing, Maggie lurches and giggles. I have been jumping these rocks since boyhood and have succeeded in making the half mile from the Point's tip to the beach in a series of leaps, never touching the pebbles between the boulders. Matthew is too young for these acrobatics, though when he was Maggie's size, he, too, giggled when I put him aloft and set off. I hear an anguished "Daddy" behind me and turn to see poor Matthew foundering between some rocks. A roll of fog turns the color of his clothes to a uniform gray-white. As I retrace our jumps back to him, the fog has thickened so much that we can no longer see the roof of our house. At the same time, a hole appears in the whiteness just to the right of where I think our house should be, and through it I see the dark side of another house. I gasp in surprise. I know that it is my uncle's house, but for that one moment through the fog, I was reminded of another house that once stood there.

When I was a boy, the little house that is now ours did not exist. The space it occupies was layered in poison ivy and oaks with tops clipped flat by the wind. But close by, at the end of the long driveway that passes the tennis court stood a house so big that it cast a shadow over the entire sea that was just down the winding path leading from its pillored porch. It was that house that I had glimpsed through the fog.

I feared and loved that house. Its smell is my fondest memory of it, a gentle, musky odor of salt-impregnated wood. Although dark and immense, it was also deceptively friendly looking. Its long living room was dom-

inated on one side by a great porch that overlooked the
sea and on the other side by a huge fireplace that crackled
with long log pines on fogbound days like today. A messy
desk stood in one corner, its papers containing messages of
no more urgency than the summer's racing schedule, a
wedding announcement, or an invitation to a cocktail
party. A wicker couch with squashy pillows stood at one
end of the room. As children, my cousins and I used to
snuggle in their softness. A delicate rocking chair was
nearby. That was my grandmother's chair. She was the
matriarch of the family.

The annual trek to Cape Cod was made as much to
pay homage to this lady as it was to spend some weeks beside the sea. I remember running into the house upon arriving to lay my face against her soft cheek and to nuzzle
against her great bosoms in a greeting that I never enjoyed. My grandmother hugged me once whenever I vis-
ited her, but that was all. She never played with me; she
never read to me; and she never told me stories. She kept
her distance, and I wanted to be so loved by this woman
whom all my relatives acknowledged as the leader of the
family.

I wondered why she never seemed to like me. I could
never figure out what I had done wrong except to be shy.
It never occurred to me that she might be shy of me.
Later, I realized that her view of me must have been tempered by her feelings toward her eldest son, my father. He
was the black sheep of the family, after all, the wayward
son who had decided to become a dirt farmer rather than
to enter one of the respectable professions. Her dismissal
of this occupation caused him, and thus me, to stand in
fear of her judgment.

My realization of her skepticism of me came when I
was eight or so. I had chosen not to sail in the afternoon
race, a transgression for which I felt immense guilt. I did

not race because I feared my father's wrath if I did something wrong on the boat. But on the Point, one was not supposed to regard boats with mixed emotion. One was expected to embrace them.

Full of confused shame, I moped into the big living room. My grandmother was there alone, knitting. She looked up at me and asked, "What, you're not racing?" I mumbled something about having a cold. She put her knitting down on her lap, stared at me for a full ten seconds that seemed ten minutes, and declared, "You are the strangest child I have ever met," the word "strangest" coming out in a twisted way that let me know that my case was unique, never before witnessed on Weenaumet. In my fragility, it was the final blow, delivered with stunning accuracy. But I said nothing. Though my eyes were awash in tears, I did not want her to say anything more that would reduce me to sobbing.

She was the beloved matron of the Point and with good reason. To many residents, she was known as Granny. She looked the classic Granny—from her soft wrinkled skin and big bosoms to her stooped but determined walk that took her to every part of the Point where traditions were being played out. A race brought her to the beach to greet the incoming boats; a tennis match, to the court to applaud the shots and to share news with the onlookers. On Weenaumet, the elders have always carried great respect, in some cases, the conscience of the community.

And she was beloved for her eccentricities. After a meal on a blustery evening when the fire roared in the huge fireplace, she would sidle over to the timbers, turn around, lift the back of her skirt, and a dreamy look would transform her face into smiling contentment as the heat drifted upward.

There were no rules in that house; there were traditions and expectations. After greeting my grandmother upon our annual arrival, I proceeded to the vast kitchen, where the old coal stove and refrigerator with the round cooling unit on top squatted. The two Irish servants were waiting to cluck over me, but I could barely understand their brogue. Still, I felt their warmth. I was always amazed at how the varnished woodwork of the kitchen and pantry sparkled year after year, and I swam my fingers over it. I wanted to go out to the laundry room just to sniff the hand-washed clothes and maybe crank the old wringer around a few times, but I feared that such an odd detour would be talked about.

Once on the third floor, where I would sleep, I sighed with relief. It was quiet and airy way up there, so high that no one ever bothered me. The nursery was there. It spanned the entire width of the house and was full of old-fashioned teddy bears on wheels and wooden pull toys that used to belong to my father and his brothers and sister. I found comfort in the toys but could not believe that my stern father had ever played with them. In my little bedroom down the hall from the nursery, the cast-iron bed was in its same position under the eaves. Racing pennants hung from the moldings in a colorful display of sailing prowess, though the sight of them made me nervous. I knew that if I did not win some this summer, my father would be disappointed. I felt soothed, though, when I opened the window and the southwest wind caressed me with sea smell and damp salt. It made me forget the conversation downstairs and the prospect of descending to see all my relatives.

I lingered long enough to come down toward the end of the cocktail hour. Aunts and uncles greeted me warmly with grown-up handshakes or kisses on the cheek. They told me how glad they were to see me and they offered me a Coca-Cola in a glass filled with ice, which I sipped just

like they sipped their gin and tonics or bourbons. I didn't
know what to say to them. I thought I should act grown-
up but had no idea how to be grown-up. I envied my cousins; they seemed so able to slip from childish glee to ma-
ture childhood. They had poise. I never imagined I would
have any.

When one of the servants came to the living-room
door and motioned to my grandmother that dinner was
ready, we marched into the dining room and sat at Windsor chairs with struts that dug into backs. I had a hard
time taking food from the serving dishes that the maid
brought around. I was afraid that if I dropped a utensil or
some Harvard beets, the conversation would stop and everyone would stare at me.

After dinner I quickly escaped the living-room chatter about family and community and sailing and sought
refuge in my garret with a book, though most of the time I
stared out the window at the turning beacon of the lighthouse in the bay, the wind in my face. Sometimes my
mother came up and told me it was too bad I wouldn't
stay downstairs, other members of the family would like to
get to know me. I was terrified by the idea. I feared that
whatever I might say would be met with uncomprehend-
ing eyes and that they would all just stare, waiting for me
to say something worthy of them.

My grandmother died eighteen years ago, and the
house, almost as if she had commanded it to do so from
above, burned to the ground a few months later. Though I
hated myself in that house, I will always miss the smell of
its rooms. I envision what it must have looked like going
up in flames one snowy evening, the fire trucks skidding
and finally getting stuck on the long, unplowed driveway.
The firemen in the town still shake their heads in awe at
the ferocity of the blaze. I see the salty woodwork darken
and burst into flames, the beautiful lithographs of nine-

teenth-century whaling scenes curl up in the heat, my bed melting, and a tremendous sigh of relief from everyone in the family who had worried that there would be a squabble over the house after my grandmother died.

My father and an uncle divided the land. Both sailors from childhood, they wanted houses that fit their souls. My uncle built a graceful structure on the site of his mother's house, reminiscent in two rising wings of a beached sailboat with sails still filled. My father built a tight little ship for himself, beating against the southwest wind. Open the door leading to the deck overlooking the sea and you get bowled over by the force of it. Then he ran out of money and filled the interior with knotty pine. The house is a memorial to him.

August 7

On calm, sunny days the children play on the deck overlooking the bay. They enjoy each other more now, able to laugh at each other's imagination and launch their play from the seeds of an idea. After consuming a sticky pancake breakfast, Matthew says that he wants to play with Play-Doh. Maggie, still imitative, parrots, "I wanna play do, too." Wonderfully creative but messy stuff, it too easily and too permanently ends up ground into rugs and between floorboards. We have decreed that Play-Doh is an outside activity. I rinse the maple syrup off their little dining table and carry it to the deck along with chairs and containers of different-colored Play-Doh. Matthew, now a pro with it, tackles the clay with assurance. He obviously has an object in mind. Maggie just loves to squish it between her hands.

Most of Matthew's recent projects have been undertaken with the objective of improving upon aerospace design. The thing that he now forms to his satisfaction is an obvious breakthrough, though it looks to me like a multi-colored ball with a snubby snout and two malformed projections. I am told that these are engine "arms." What he has made of course is a spaceship. It is en route to the planet Venturn, which lies in Matthew's mind somewhere between Venus and Saturn. He runs up and down the deck with his creation held overhead to show me how fast it is traveling. Maggie jumps into action holding aloft a glob of Play-Doh. "See my faceship [sic]. It go fast," and she stumbles off after her brother.

He soon abandons his craft in favor of a much more convincing-looking Transformer. This one is a three-inch-long space-shuttle model. But with a few twists and tugs it can be transformed into a ferocious-looking and heavily armed robot. I am amazed and fascinated by these revolutionary toys, and although I shrink in horror whenever I walk down the aisles of a Toys-R-Us store, I have to admire the mind of the person who thought of taking an old-fashioned kind of toy like a car, truck, or airplane and putting a laser weapon in a headlight, a rocket launcher in a wheel, or a robot's head in an engine block. The two-facedness of these toys make them a convenient tool for indoctrinating young minds to a recently ingrained truism—that what seems to be is not what is. Matthew enjoys the duplicity by crowing the Transformer code song: "Transformers in the sky/more than meets the eye"; a very apt ditty whose meaning some tender child has undoubtedly probed and, upon understanding, has suddenly turned wiser and less trusting.

His eyes dancing with delight, Matthew launches the shuttle for my benefit and accompanies it on tiptoe to the stars. Then in a flash, he transforms it into a robot and alters his personality to fit its ugliness. "I'm going to kill you guys with my laser beam," he crows and zaps Maggie and me with crashing sounds. I scowl as I usually do when Matthew turns violent, and offer some meaningful but trite advice that gentleness is more lasting than brute strength. My surprise is that he often responds by calming down, his violence dwindling to a story about a trip to another planet where green people who eat pancakes live.

I think he is relieved when Willa and I tell him not to be violent. It is not really part of his nature, only a behavior that his experience with schoolmates leads him to think he should indulge in. *Sesame Street* and *Mr. Rogers* satisfy him. He never asks to see the violent children's TV shows, though his preschool teacher is amazed that he knows all the characters so well. He learns their personalities, motivations, and movements by picking up other children's renditions of them, a feat that I find incredible. As evidence of the ephemeral nature of any violent streak he might possess, he recently asked me after he had mowed down a bunch of bad guys with a laser gun: "Daddy, are guns as strong as the wind that blows sailboats through the water?"

Maggie ignores her brother's roughness. She returns to her Play-Doh and makes a pancake. Her activity offers Matthew an opportunity to keep face. He pretends to pour maple syrup over it, and the two of them begin play-eating it, ripping the flattened shape to shreds and growling like little animals.

I pick up a book, but the scene before me—children playing, dazzling day, water lapping on the rocks, and gliding flights of gulls—makes me put it down. Whenever I watch the children play in harmony, I think about where they have come from. Colic tortured Matthew during his first three months of life and made a squalling terror of him. His digestive tract was not well enough developed to tolerate even mother's milk. Whatever went into his stomach sent his little body writhing in pain.

He was born on the edge of prematurity, five weeks early. Colic is common in such cases, doctors told us. A condition that cures itself with time, its only medications are sympathy and patience. But sympathy is sometimes hard to find. Though Willa and I felt sorry for this bundle of agony, his constant screaming and our loss of sleep led us only to tolerate him while guiltily holding back our love until his stomach grew up.

At the time, I was helping to launch a new magazine (a full-time job) and renovating an old house that we purchased a week after Matthew's birth, an unwise time, to be sure, but the price was right. Those months were so difficult that I have truly forgotten how bad they were. I remember arising at 5:30 every morning. The house was half an hour by subway from where we were living. I had just enough time to go there to let in and direct the carpenters, plumbers, and electricians before plunging back into the subway to get to the office. Immediately after leaving the magazine for the day, I would return to the house and begin working on it myself—tearing down old walls, erecting new ones, painting, and so on. It was close to midnight when I arrived back at our apartment to find Willa red-eyed and groggy and Matthew screaming.

I had it easy. Willa suffered far more. To be trapped in an apartment with a screaming and inconsolable baby is a torture that only parents with colicky newborns can understand. We lived in bewilderment; one moment, he was a helpless thing; the next, a thrashing demon. I felt like a rotten father, a rotten husband, a rotten editor. I wondered in my more clear-headed moments why I should be paid for my work when I was only half-conscious of what I was doing. But the gutted house had to have floors and rooms, lights and comfort, before we could move in, and the lease on our apartment was due to expire. Rationalizations aside, guilt riddled and almost smothered me when I arrived home, exhausted, to be handed a screaming Matthew. Selfishly, I was angry at Willa for not seeing my exhaustion, then angered by my anger, then angry at Matthew for not shutting up, then guilty for not acknowledging that the cause of the problem was a tiny stomach out in the world before its time. As the tension mounted, Matthew's screaming grew louder.

When the house could finally be left to the workmen, and the flow of articles at the magazine was under control, we escaped to Jamaica for a week. Matthew was just three months old. I jumped out of bed the first morning after our arrival, alarmed that he was not screaming. He was lying on his back in his playpen staring out the window at huge tropical leaves dancing in the breeze. When he noticed me, a grin broke across his face. He smiled, ate, and slept during that entire week, and we heard not a scream from him.

We had been told to expect this—the sudden cessation of the screaming when his digestive tract matured enough to handle food—but we had not believed it possible. As relieved as we were, we also wondered if the sudden quiet might be an indication that Matthew was sick. But we were soon able to laugh at our ceaseless worry, realizing that it came out of a love and concern that could only grow with our child.

Our consciousness of the daily horror of Matthew's colic quickly dimmed, but it will always be with us. It colored Willa's pregnancy with Maggie two years after. We feared a repetition. When Maggie came into the world smiling and sleeping the night through, we were stunned. She was the stereotypical ideal baby who ate when she was supposed to, burped on cue, smiled at our friends, and charmed the world with enormous eyes.

She is even more charming now. I must resist the urge to sweep her from the floor and endlessly squeeze her in great bear hugs, which she returns by clasping her little arms around my neck. But in this stage of her life, she is as full of squawks and whines as of clowning and delight. The hugs she loves to accept when she is in a good mood become her obsession in a foul one. This morning she awakened in a "I wanna hug" mood. I heard her calling from her room just as the sun rose, a drawn-out "Dad-deee" wail, repeated every few seconds and increasing in squawkiness with each repetition. I went to her room. I knew that if I didn't, her racket would awaken Willa and Matthew. She was lying on her back in her bed, her head raised regally on her pillow, her chestnut tresses flowing out on either side. Looking at me defiantly with her thumb stuck in her mouth, she demanded a hug, no questions asked. I hesitated a second too long. "I WANNA HUG," she yelled. I knew that she was speaking obliquely; she wanted to cling to me much more than she wanted a hug. And a clinging Maggie meant that I could not make coffee, get breakfast for the children, the dog, the daddy, wash my face, shave, read the newspaper, and so forth. If the world were all Maggie's, I would be hugging her all day. On such mornings, I give her a nice hug and quickly change the subject.

"Maggie, did you have any nice dreams?"

"No."

"Let's have breakfast, Mag. How about scrambled eggs?"

"No."

"How about Cheerios with peaches?"

"No."

"How about pancakes?"

"No."

"How about fried sea horses and cucumber toast?"

"No."

"Well, what do you want for breakfast, Maggie?"

"I wanna hug."

Fifteen minutes later I persuaded her to swallow half a dozen Cheerios. Not much, but it eased the hunger pangs. She got up from her little table and climbed onto a chair next to mine at the dining table. She had her eyes on my toast. Another morning ritual had begun. "I wanna taste."

"I'll get some toast for you, Maggie," I offered.

"No, I wanna taste."

"Look, I'll get you your very own piece, just for Maggie."

"Yours, I wanna taste toast yours."

I broke off a little piece. She chewed it, and her mood suddenly did an about-face with her standing on the chair and doing a little dance. "Maggie, sit down," I said. "You'll fall; that's very dangerous."

She stopped, and her big moon eyes stared down at me. She smiled and said, "I bigger than you now."

August 8

The beach here is no more than a spot of sand lining an inlet's shore and bordered by jetties and wharves at each end. Just off the longer of the two jetties, Herreschoffs, Bulleyes, Widgeons, and occasional chubby inboards are moored, small craft whose bobbing in the wash of passing stinkpots sporting flying bridges and fish rods suggests a threatened innocence.

At low tide, the eelgrass and mud begin just a few feet from the water's edge, discouraging swimmers. But high tide brings the water six feet up the beach, the sand beneath giving it a green cast. Then the beach becomes a stage. Families with small children descend upon it by bicycle and foot and in cars from which rubber rafts and plastic sea monsters protrude. Each family tends to take an accustomed place—some using the stones of one jetty for backrests, others plunking down in the middle of the sand, their headquarters a weathered bench with a slanting roof. Repetition is the stuff of this place. People can be found in exactly the same spot from one year to the next. In the midst of a dreary winter's day in New York, I warm myself with a daydream of summers on the Point and invariably settle on the comforting vision of someone on his or her particular pile of sand.

Today, with the sun bright, the tide reaching a mid-morning high, and children yammering to go swimming, we take our place among the families, usually in the same spot in front of the covered bench. The car is only half unloaded, but already a pile of equipment holds down the beach towels: Styrofoam containers full of peanut butter and jelly sandwiches and apple juice, life preservers, a fat inflatable raft, books, minnow nets, and Maggie's "Dolly Kateen," named in honor of a long-gone baby-sitter. At least four trips back to the car are required to empty it. In talk that has been repeated many times, families with small children compare notes on how much stuff they cram into their vehicles for even a short stay on the beach.

At water's edge, wind surfers ready their crafts. On the long jetty a couple of old salts stand chatting, the wind whipping their yellow slickers and flattening khaki pants against lean legs. No one has to guess at their conversation; boats are their lives, and sailing, nautical technology, and racing their daily fare. On Saturday afternoons this jetty is *the* meeting place for racers after they have put away their boats. Their conversations are repetitions of ones held last summer, or five summers ago—of luffing matches, claims of buoy room, of tense spinnaker runs and little-known currents.

Behind us, an older woman sits on the covered bench and, as she does every day, surveys the scene. Children run up to show off their treasures to her—shells, beach toys, half-eaten sandwiches—anything that they hold dear, depending upon their age. Soon to become the matriarch of the community, she keeps tabs on how much each child has grown from one summer to the next. Her mere presence instills a sense of tradition. Her mother once assumed the same role, the splinterly bench her throne, a straw hat clasped to her head by a broad blue ribbon her crown. Young parents gathered around this figurehead to show her their offspring as a way of assuring her and themselves that when she died, the place would continue to be inhabited by children of old blood. My grandmother preceded this woman as the benevolent matriarch of Weenaumet, her wrinkled and deep-set eyes squinting against sun and sand, her flattened hand raised to brow as a shield against the brilliance. She, above all, was the guardian of tradition, cherishing those who maintained it, chastising those who threatened it.

Behind the beach, a little tidal pond connects to the ocean via a twisting, grass-lined creek. Twice each day, a torrent of water surges through the creek and into the pond, and twice each day the same water rampages out, carrying a myriad of tiny fish, shrimp, shellfish, and occasional eels. Children are forever wading up and down the creek with minnow nets in hand to prey upon this bounty. They grow up knowing that the little ecosystem is the source of all life.

After swimming, Matthew and I go over to the creek. Fiddler crabs scuttle toward their holes, exhibiting a ridiculous display of disequilibrium with their one enormous and one tiny claw. The tide is just turning, the current flowing gently seaward. Matthew wades in with care, though the water is clear. Spider crabs hide in the algae that clings to rocks on the bottom. I understand his hesitation but try to assure him that these crabs are harmless, their pincers barely big enough to grasp a reed. I do warn him, though, of blue claws. When I was a boy, blue claws obsessed one of the nannies who took care of cousins in my grandmother's house. During her off hours, she scurried to the tidal pond bearing a long-handled crab net and crept along its edges in search of the crabs. The creatures she hauled out terrified me, with their thrashing claws searching for fingers or toes to mutilate. Even now, I am alert to the presence of the crabs and I am glad that Matthew is cautious.

A passing school of minnows diverts his fear, but he brings his net up empty. We work our way downstream trying to corner young menhaden in the shallows. Whenever I have a netful of squirming minnows, he runs over and demands to hold each one, staring at their glistening flanks with a rapture that comes, I suppose, from holding a complete life in the palm of your hand.

There is something about the tidal pond and its creek that casts a spell over the people here. In the peace that often descends over the Point just before sunset, the air clears of its midday haze and brings the surrounding marsh grass into focus, making a mirror of the pond framed by green-yellow marsh grass so motionless as to be suspended in time. Residents sometimes come to the pond's edge to breathe in the suspension. They say very little; with long gazes and furrowed brows, they view a work of art.

One fall, after the children had left the tidal pond to return to their winter homes, a resident took it upon himself to enlarge the beach's parking area by dumping a truckload of gravel on the marsh grass. His neighbors, an unabusive group of people, heaped scorn upon him, not by railing against him but by a more condemnatory means: They ignored him. Greetings on the beach and waves upon the road were held back, cocktail party invitations were no longer placed in his mailbox, blank faces met his beseeching looks. The man stood alone upon the beach staring out to sea in confusion that a mere truckload of gravel had reduced his position in the community to a pile of rubble.

A consciousness of fragility sharpens the atmosphere

here, an awareness that the Point's long peace hovers on the edge of ruin. Anchor lines are beginning to chafe. The place once seemed so secure in its removal from the mainstream, grounded on large families whose sons went to Harvard and whose daughters married Harvard men. The framework for change was unwittingly laid by the original settlers. Quietly proud of their means to establish huge houses by the sea and to hire the help necessary to maintain them, they propagated child after child to be raised by nannies and sent to private schools. These children— the heirs—have now grown old and wiry, and their comfortable family wealth has diminished. Their offspring, whose numbers are only slightly less than those of their parents' generation, have their own children to support and no longer live within an hour's drive of Weenaumet. The shared fear here is that a storm of change will whip up as the old-timers die off, leaving their unmanageable houses and expansive acreages to distant children who do not have the means or inclination to keep them up.

Whether these older people have survived the winter is a matter of open curiosity at the beginning of each summer. One does not initially ask overt questions. One looks for signs—the familiar sight of a stooped figure means survival, a certain boat missing from her mooring may signal an unhappy occurrence during a cold winter's evening.

The storm of change is being fueled by the demands of the outside world and its willingness to put down absurd sums of money for waterfront property. The pittance the original settlers paid for shore frontage has now grown to $100,000 an acre. The big houses with their ten bedrooms and wonderful sea smells are now worth millions of dollars. Not all members of the younger generation want to perpetuate tradition. They would much rather have their money. Family feuds are beginning to simmer as some siblings demand to sell while others plead to stay.

Bulldozers are becoming a common sight here. They rip driveways through the catbrier and poison ivy to provide access for energy-efficient homes whose sites have been carved out of larger holdings that have fallen into dispute. Who is building these houses? How will they change the Point's embedded flavor? More threatening are the new people who can afford to purchase one of the old weathered homes, people with unusual-sounding last names. My uncle refers to their imminent arrival as the coming of the Texans. "Some Texan might buy one of these houses and change this place overnight," he says somberly.

Unknowns have never been greeted with warmth here—another tradition. As a child, I was impressed by my grandmother's adamant rejection of any unpedigreed newcomer and her wrath at established families who would dare sell. When the daughter of one of the original settlers sold a few acres to people who constructed a glistening white cube, my grandmother's irritations included buyer as well as seller. "A shoebox," she called the house, "lived in by a doctor nobody knows. I don't know what the place is coming to." She would have preferred that the land had been sold to a Boston family with a recognized name, people that she liked to call "old shoes."

One of the old houses did recently fall to some unknowns. Breaths were held as the family moved in, the question on everyone's lips, "Is this the end of the Point as we have known it?" When the newcomers hosted a party with a rock band that one beautiful moonlit night blasted music the length of the community, audible sighs were heard expelled among the pitch pines. "Aha," the whispers went, "so this is how the end is to be."

But the old guard still has fight. Leaders of the community invited the transgressor to a gathering of residents at which it was announced that the man had promised (a promise given at a private meeting beforehand) never to disturb the tranquillity again. A show was made of forgiving and welcoming him to traditional ways. But it rang hollow; the affront had been too great. Yet this man has caused no further ill will. Only two or three residents have spoken to him since that incident. He and his family, shipwrecked foreigners on a furtively watched island, must wait their turn for acceptance, as the guardians of tradition die off one by one.

August 9

Matthew gave me a dandelion today. I was reading on the deck when he came to me with it in outstretched hand. Very solemn in his presentation, he said, "Here, Dada, look at what I found. This is for you." I thanked him just as solemnly. He stared at me, waiting, his lips bearing just a slight smile and his eyes just a little crinkled. His hair is always tousled; his head was perched forward, his shoulders squared. His awkwardness made me realize how fast he is growing, too fast for his bones.

I love his face. His lips are thick, particularly the lower one. When he speaks, they move exaggeratedly and draw your eyes to them. Willa thinks the lower lip is marvelously sexy. I like his eyes the most, cat eyes. Almost almond-shaped, they are as smiling as his mouth. Their color is dazzling, the perimeter of the iris a dark brown that circles a band of gray-yellow, segmented by tiny vertical black stripes. Inside, a ring of aqua-green sets off, finally, the black pupil.

"What are you going to do with the flower, Dada?" he asked, breaking my reverie. "You better put it in a glass of water."

But I told him that instead I would put it into the

pocket of my shirt so that I would be able to look at it whenever I wanted to. He watched me insert the stem into the pocket and adjust the blossom so that it peered out nicely over the edge. "That looks nice, Dada. I'm going swinging now. Bye." He wheeled and ran below the deck to where we hung the kids' swings, his long brown legs with their huge knees flashing out of sight.

That afternoon I haul the old sailfish out. It has not been used in two years, propped during that period against a horse stable in my grandmother's garage. The garage escaped the fire. Now my uncle's and my family store boats in it. During winters, it is crammed with hulls of various shapes and sizes. On spring weekends, it smells of sanded paint and varnish as members of the family ready their boats for summer. During summers, it is deserted, save for a few ignored craft.

When my father was a boy, he and his brothers and sister used to play in the garage. They had a clubhouse in one of its closets, and over the door they nailed a sign that, still in place, bears the warning: DANGER, DO NOT ENTER. They slung ropes from the rafters and swung from one side of the structure to the other, undoubtedly scaring the horses half to death. There's my father as a boy again, pursuing, as he must have in the nursery, boyish activities. I am able to accept his childhood only as an intellectual fact. My knowledge of him as an adult makes me unable to see the possibility of a child's joy within him.

They must have irritated Gilbert. Gilbert was the caretaker. He lived in a six-by-ten-foot room off the garage, the room where I am writing these words. I know only selected details of his life on Weenaumet. He left no evidence of his stay here, not a smudge on the wall from a kerosene lamp or an old newspaper on a shelf or even markings on the floor to suggest where his bed might have scraped it. I share his former dwelling with only a couple of torn tennis court nets heaped upon the floor and a pair of long-abandoned oars. His little room was undoubtedly stifling on a windless summer's night. I picture him sitting outside the garage in the evening trying to feel some fingers of breeze playing on the sea two hundred yards away.

One of his daytime chores must have been to polish the model Ts that occupied the garage. A tire that he changed is still here, crumpled up in my father's clubhouse next to the one-holer, under which mushrooms now proliferate.

Older members of my family tell me that he was a lady's man. In former days, the beach was given over to the summer staff between two and four every afternoon, a noble gesture on the part of their employers, who could have insisted that they swim off the rocks in the front of the houses. Caretakers, chauffeurs, cooks, maids, nannies, and other employees would gather on the beach to play among the nautical toys of richer men. Gilbert, an exuberant man, took to tossing the female help into the water from the dock, and eventually the screams of delight disturbed the Point's customary repose. Mistresses and masters complained to my grandparents. I can imagine Gilbert relegated to his little room as punishment.

The sailfish, coated in dust, is far removed from its sleek appearance thirty years ago, when my father constructed it from thousands of pieces of wood. Its light green deck is pitted and scratched, its varnished sides flaking. Worse, the compound that concealed screw heads has worked loose, exposing the raw wood inside to rot and the corrosive effects of salt water. My father made the hull in his spare time over the course of an entire winter. I marveled at the symmetry of the ribs before he glued on the perfectly curved sides and bottom. Every rib of that boat had to be aligned just so and every support sanded and resanded until all the pieces fit together like a jigsaw puzzle. I remember him eyeing the finished hull, never a smile, always critical, especially of himself. But I was proud of him and happy that what had seemed an incomprehensible jumble of sticks and boards had come together with such order. Perfection was the least my father expected of himself and others. As such rigor lies mostly in the mind of the beholder, the completion of projects left him perpetually dissatisfied.

When I was six or seven, he started me off on carpentry by teaching me how to build a wooden box. "If you can't build a box square," he told me, "you can't build anything." We went to the local lumberyard and bought some cedar planks, soft and easily worked wood. The box was to be the size of a shoebox. He taught me how to join the edges in a strong bond and how to cut the top for a perfect fit. But the box was far from perfect. Though every joint looked true and tight and all the angles were ninety degrees, the box rocked back and forth as if it had an invisible fulcrum beneath it. I planed and sanded the bottom, but it still rocked, and the more I worked on it, the worse the imbalance grew. Nevertheless, I was proud of my work. I wanted to take it to my bedroom and fill it with treasures. But every time my father examined it, he scowled and said, "You didn't get something square. You will never be a good builder unless you can get everything square." At last he gave up scowling and never said anything more about the box. I kept odds and ends in it for years, feeling a certain affection for it each time I lifted the top, although never far away was a picture of my father's disapproving look.

Later I built a boat, again under his hard gaze. I had an idea of the kind of boat I wanted to build, something along the lines of the punt that Pogo poled around his swamp. When I set to, my father chose the moment to inform me that boat building presented the most difficult carpentry possible. Discouraged (not by this information but by the realization that my progress was to be monitored and judged all the way) but not defeated, I cut and nailed together the planks. The finished product was homegrown to say the least, about five feet long, two feet wide, and weighed close to one hundred pounds. When I put it in the water, little geysers erupted at every joint. I was not surprised. By that time, I had become so accustomed to my father's criticisms that a voice within had warned me to expect little from my labors. Fortunately, I was always aware of another voice, and I do not know where it came from, telling me never to give up.

My father built the sailfish at a time when a sailfish craze gripped the community. Weekend races turned the bay into a rainbow of colored sails. Between races, they lined the shore, rhythmically bobbing up and down as waves lifted under the beached craft. After each race, I listened raptly to the harrowing experiences of the racers, of capsizing and righting downed craft until exhaustion set in, of flipping bow over stern on a downwind leg. My father never won a race, though he tried and tried. Eventually, he abandoned the boat, the thought apparently never crossing his mind that one could have fun with her, nosing around the bay.

One summer I was told I was big enough to race the sailfish. I was terrified by the prospect and made up excuses—a tennis match, a cold, a book I wanted to read. My father looked at me queerly, as if I were a stranger. Sometimes I was more honest and merely said that I did not wish to race. Then my father would frown and shrug and turn away. My heart grew heavy and sank. Though in most areas I could numb myself to his criticism, I could not ignore it when it came to boats, knowing that sailing was closest to my father's reason for living. The knowledge drove through me like a dagger, the pain a silent recognition that I wanted to please him.

After I had worn out all the excuses, I decided to race. The wind was bellowing out of the southwest. Fifteen sailfish beat to windward, and I quickly fell into last place. The boat would not move. Her bow plunged into each wave, stopping her dead. I panicked and thought of all the people watching and shaking their heads at this sorry display taking place in their waters. I thought about it so much that I quickly lost any ability to maneuver the boat. I capsized her, and after righting her and hauling myself on board, she capsized again, and again. Waves rolled her over so that her sail hung straight down in the water. Each time I began to right her, every muscle in my body strained. My chest was a patchwork of bruises from pulling myself up on the deck.

Out of the corner of my eye, I could see a launch approach. My father peered down at me. "Come on, old man [his nickname for me]," he said rather kindly, "you've had enough." And he hauled me out of the water as one would grasp a drowning cat. I expected judgments to rain down upon me, but he said not a word. No one said a word. I wanted my failure out in the open, but silence was all I heard.

I spend the afternoon patching the paint, applying varnish, and filling in the screw holes. Now I look at the boat as a toy. It makes no difference to me whether I can race her or not. I don't care whether she sails fast or slow. All I have ever really wanted from her is the pleasure of allowing me to slice through the water. But at this moment I want her for something else—to teach Matthew the same joy. Racing can come later, if he is so inclined.

Toward evening, we take the boat down to the beach and rig her. Age and abandonment have warped the centerboard; it will not go down all the way. The rudder is loose. No mind. The wind is not strong, and Matthew is eager to go. Unlike me at that age, fear of the boat is only an awareness in the back of his mind. He snaps on his "bubble," the Styrofoam blob that keeps him afloat, and jumps onto the deck. We churn away from the beach on a broad reach. Waves break over the deck, and Matthew grins from ear to ear. I tell him to hang on tight to the top of the protruding centerboard and to the boat's meager railings. He does so by lying down on the deck and curling his body around the centerboard so that he is one with the rise and fall and heel of the boat.

August 10

Mornings are like tornadoes. This morning the storm, as usual, begins in Maggie's little corner room. A light sleeper, she awakens to the sunrise chatter of red squirrels, the alarm cry of crows, and the surprised-sounding complaints of gulls sweeping over the house.

"Daddee, com'ere," begins the storm. Now, Maggie is a slight child, smaller than most two-and-a-half-year-olds. I love to watch her march around the house dressed in just a pair of shorts. Her skinny legs, unsure at times of the direction of her march, angle off in crazy directions before catching up with the momentum of her body. Her shoulders, absurdly square, look powerful against her long, delicate neck and her terribly flat chest. Her chest has no discernible muscles whatsoever, leaving an impression of helpless innocence, exacerbated by a ridiculous body that bulges over the waistband of her shorts.

But behind all that innocence and charm lies a set of lungs with the capacity to send Brio, the puppy, scampering behind the sofa. The wails grow with each half second that I do not appear at her bedside. I go to her as fast as possible in the futile hope that I can again shut up her racket before it awakens Matthew and Willa—though I am not too worried about Willa, who has taken to wearing earplugs the night through.

A large part of my haste is made out of the selfish desire to be the best father I can. Matthew needs his sleep; with less than eleven hours, he dissolves into a miniature monster with a whine as tenacious as Maggie's wail. If I get to Maggie's room in time, Matthew will get enough sleep, and I can be a decent father.

I push open Maggie's door. She is lying on her back, tears streaming down her face. They are, of course, crocodile tears. Everything about her has turned crocodilian, though she can still be charming.

"Daddee," she wails. "I no go to sleep." The storm is strengthening.

"No, Maggie," I say. "It's morning. Did you have nice dreams?"

"No," she blurts out. "I no go to sleep. Where's Mat'ew?"

"Matthew's sleeping, so let's be quiet. Shh."

"Where's Mommy?"

"Mommy's sleeping. Shh."

"Where's Brio?" Brio makes her entrance on cue and grabs Maggie's Dolly Kateen by the hair and gives it a shake and rakes her paws over its body. Maggie explodes. "No, Brio; No, Brio," she yells in her hoarse voice of utter frustration. "You le'go Dolly Kateen." She collapses back onto the pillow in a fit of sobs. I swat the dog and grab the doll and put it beside Maggie and change the subject, my ears tuned for an outcry from Matthew's room. I steel myself for the approach of a maelstrom by thinking that I will look back on this phase of child rearing with tears of amusement in my eyes.

"I did do-do." Maggie wails and then repeats her

announcement in a raised voice for special effect.

"Okay, let's change you."

"No change me. I wan' cheer-weers [Cheerios]."

"No, Maggie. I have to change you first, then let's get dressed, and then we'll eat Cheerios." She looks up at me, a pool of tears in each eye and her lower lip puffed out, her characteristic acknowledgment of total defeat. I take off her diaper, and there is truly a mess underneath, which requires a good two dozen tissues and a dozen moistened paper towels to clean up. While doing so I have to fend off Brio, who is executing her morning playfulness with nips to Maggie's feet. It occurs to me once again that the acquisition of this dog was premature. Matthew plays with her only at his convenience, and Maggie is so perturbed by the constant nipping that she warns the dog away with one of her "No, Brio!" rasps even when the poor animal is out of sight.

Finally, I get up and carry the dog out of the room and close the door, but Maggie screams, "No close door! No close door."

Partially defeated myself, and it is not even seven o'clock, I say sarcastically, "Sure, Maggie. Okay, whatever you want," and open the door. Brio bounds in.

"No, Brio. Go 'way. No, Brio!" I find that at times like this my mind locks into a drive position. A job remains to be done, one with extraordinary obstacles that could make a less resolute person wash his hands of the entire matter and awaken the children's mother, pleading an immediate need to go to the supermarket for a gallon of milk.

"Okay, Maggie," I say authoritatively but with a slight singsong in my voice that I trust will soothe a demon. "Let's get dressed. I'm going to try to find some underpants for you." I start tossing around clothes to find what I want. The shelf of her closet where her clothes are kept is piled with shirts, pants, shorts, and so on, most of which she will not wear. But there are no underpants.

"No pants," is the expected response. "Don' put pants."

"Well, what do you want to wear?"

"I wear dress."

"Okay, but first we have to put on underpants." My voice lightens as I drag a pair out from under a pile of shirts.

"No, no pants. " I ignore her screams and force them on, wondering if she will develop a lifelong complex about wearing underpants. I decide to risk it.

"There. Now, do you want to wear this dress or this one. You tell me." I have opened her closet doors. From her bed, she can gaze upon her wardrobe of six dresses.

She points to a flowered print sundress with tie shoulder straps, a good choice, for the day promises to be hot. I take it off the hanger.

"No, dat one." She now points to a cute party dress that we bought for her a year earlier in France, adorable but a bit too fancy for the turmoil that I know we are about to enter the next phase of the morning's storm. I can't help thinking that the older generation handed their kiddies over to nannies, a blessed institution if ever there was one. I doubt if my grandmother ever had to deal with her children's fickleness; or, if a child's mood changed for the worse, a nanny could always be summoned to remove the squirming thing from earshot.

I *know* that my grandfather never changed a diaper. The only other thing I know about his treatment of his children was his method of teaching them to swim: He tied a rope around a child's waist, and if the child did not jump from the dock, he pushed. Learning to swim was, then, not quite a sink-or-swim proposition. It was swim if you could, and if you began to drown, you'd be hauled in like a fish. Though everyone in my family has swum, I have noticed that none, for all the emphasis placed on sailing, has very readily taken to the water.

Maggie changes her mind a few more times. In the midst of her decision making, "cheer-weers" comes up again, and I hasten the dressing process by slipping her first choice over her head while ignoring her squalling protests so that we can get on to the second leg of the morning ritual—eating breakfast.

"Maggie, do you want an egg for breakfast?" I ask.

"No, I wan' cheer-weers."

"Okay, how about a cut-up peach on them?"

"No, I wan' candy on t'em."

"No, Mag, no candy today. You have to wait until Friday." Friday is the only day that the children are permitted candy, and if we forget to buy it, Matthew is sure to remind us on Saturday.

"I have peach." I am momentarily stunned by her acquiescence and give her a few Cheerios so that she will stay content while I pour the cereal into a bowl and cut up a peach. She is watching. "I wan' peach here. HERE!" She slams her little hand on the table. I gather that she wants it in another bowl beside her cereal bowl. I am right. She begins eating. All is quiet. It is the eye of the morning storm.

When I prepare a meal for the children, I remind myself of short-order cooks I have observed, their hands moving in ten directions at once, leaving bacon frying to butter toast to pour coffee to squeeze orange juice, movements that look unfinished until all the ingredients suddenly appear on the table in a final flurry.

Matthew comes out of his room, sleepy-eyed and with the ends of his pajama legs scuffing under his feet. He leans against my legs and hugs them. He slumps and stays there clinging. I know it's a waking-up game.

"Matthew, what did you dream about last night?" I ask.

"Pirates," he mumbles.

"Did they find any treasure?"

"Yes, they found it right there." He is wide awake and pointing toward the shore in front of the house. "They came in the night and I heard them and do you know what, there was one that didn't have one arm."

"What did they do with the treasure?" He looks up at me, and his eyes crinkle.

"Oh, they took it to Africa and got some elephants."

"What did they want elephants for?"

"They wanted to ride them, and do you know what?"

"What?"

"They could fly."

"Fly?" I ask amazed.

"Yes; they fly at Christmas and give presents to all the children." Recounting a dream has become a garbled version of one of Babar's adventures. I ask Matthew what he wants for breakfast.

"I think I want an ostrich egg." I suggest that he begin calling up his friends and ask them over for an ostrich-egg breakfast party.

We joke back and forth. I feel a lovely softness inside me. Finally, Matthew says that he will settle for a lobster claw. At the mention of lobster, Maggie perks up. She saw her first lobster a few days ago during a visit to a fish market, where there were hundreds of them in a tank. Maggie raised a ruckus. She wanted to touch each one. When I picked up one from the tank, she tried to wrap her tiny hand around it but let me drop it back into the tank when it moved its claws. Now the primitive creatures fascinate her.

"I wanna lob'er," she demands. But she knows that Matthew is not serious, so she returns to her cereal.

Matthew finally decides upon the usual, a mix of every kind of cereal we have with a cut-up peach on top. I begin the process, regretting my bribe of several months earlier. One morning Matthew refused to eat his Cheerios after saying that was what he wanted. I told him that he might like them better if he added some Wheaties. That worked. The next morning he wanted Cheerios, Wheaties, and Rice Crispies. Now we are up to five cereals. Something called Kix is one of them, little round plastic-looking balls of corn, which the kids adore. I make sure this morning that I add some Kix, but when I present the bowl to Matthew, he doesn't see them and cries out, "Where are the Kix?"

Maggie raises her head from her bowl, where she has been picking at dry Cheerios with her fingers. I tried to pour some milk in the bowl, but my attempt was met with howls. We worry about her lack of calcium intake and wonder if we are raising a child who will have toothpick bones.

The predictable comes out as a yell: "I wan' Kix. Give me Kix."

I give her some. "Thank you, Daddy," she chirps and looks up at me with the ends of her two upper teeth shining between her lips. I breathe a sigh. I know that the worst is over and the best is just around the corner. Matthew will gobble down his breakfast. I will have to work on him to drink his glass of milk, but he will eventually finish it. Maggie will continue to pick at her cereal. I will make myself some coffee and toast, and as soon as I sit down, she will come up to me and say, "I wanna taste toast." I will be charmed, and knowing that, she will bat her big eyes at me and lean up against me. She will singsong her request, and when I break off a little piece, she will singsong, "Thank you, Daddy," and do a little dance as she munches it. She will say proudly, "See, I dancing, I dancing. Look me dancing." Then she will come up to me and snuggle against my arm as I try to drink my coffee and say, "Daddy, I love you."

August 11

I like to introduce the children to the same experiences. But I find that one or the other inevitably gives me a bored stare or, worse, does not even respond to my invitation to look and to learn. The reason why one child reacts and the other does not has much to do with a basic difference between boys and girls, even when they are more or less the same age.

In the wake of the feminist movement, psychologists jumped on parents for tampering with their children's natural inclinations. Some psychologists accused parents of subtly treating boys and girls differently. Boys were given toys with moving parts and were encouraged to take part in competitive games. Girls had to make do with dolls and tea sets. They grew up nicely socialized but incapable of dealing with the corporate pressure cooker. As a result, in later years, boys got all the fun and important jobs. That they were emotionally retarded was not considered important.

Now, dolls for boys are suddenly acceptable. I am hearing the message through the parental grapevine that the way to encourage boys to free their emotions is to raise them more like girls. While a lot of good might come out of giving Erector sets to girls and dolls to boys, the motivations behind boys' and girls' behavior appear to be more complex than pop-psychological notions give credit.

Matthew has tried to understand how wind-up toys work since he was two years old. Then he sat on the floor, little legs outstretched, furiously pulling apart a truck or a steam engine. If he ever succeeded in exposing its innards, he would studiously examine the wheels for minute upon minute. The discovery of a battery inside a toy was sure to produce tears. Batteries make no sense to a two-year-old. Their inert form carries no possibility of discovering the force within. But when he was three, Matthew began to look upon batteries as miniature gods whose power was too mysterious to understand. By now, his adoration has disappeared. Like an adult, he doesn't even give a thought to them; he just recognizes them as objects of convenience. Maggie has not suffered Matthew's initial frustration over batteries. She has never been much for mechanical toys of any sort, save a little bee that flaps its wings when she pulls it behind her. Her affection for dolls began when she was less than a year old and has steadily grown. She is considerate of their needs, getting upset when their shoes fall off, washing them when they get dirty, and tucking them into bed.

As I wrote earlier, dirt bothers her, which is another common difference between little boys and little girls. We tell Maggie that she should go and play in the dirt, that pushing it around with your hands can feel good. She heeds our advice and sits on the ground to rub her hands in the dirt. After a few seconds she turns them palm up and stares at them. A stricken look crosses her face. We roll our eyes and hope this is just a phase.

Today, I am reminded of the differences in the two children. In the morning, we went down to the rocks in front of the house to build a fort. Instead, we were distracted by a large horseshoe crab. The prehistoric animals are common here, and the beach is littered with their broken shells, tails, and legs. But this one was still alive, its barnacled back glistening as it struggled to keep itself right side up as little waves broke over it. As accustomed as I am to seeing the crabs, they do look as if they are not of this planet. In their presence, I feel an uncertainty come over me, as if their strange shape must incorporate some powers not possessed by mammals, birds, or fish. I circled this creature, embarrassed by my wariness. Matthew was excited, Maggie contemplative.

"Turn him over, Dad. Turn him over. I want to see how he works," Matthew yelped.

Maggie stared at him, surprised at his excitement. I thought it would be educational to see how the crab "worked," so I flipped it over with a stick. Matthew grabbed the stick and began poking at the flaying legs. I told him to be gentle. Maggie repeated my request. But Matthew was not to be deterred.

"I want to see what's underneath the legs. What makes them move? Dad, do horsecrabs [sic] have a head?" I pointed out the hairy mouthparts that could give the most hardened criminal a nightmare and informed him that the head must be around there somewhere.

He bent over for a close look. "Dad, can we feed him something? I want to see how he eats."

I have no idea what Maggie thought of all this. For five minutes she quietly and unmovingly stared at the scene before her, shifting her glance between Matthew's antics and the creature's thrashing. I knew that she was thinking something; otherwise, her attention would have wandered.

Suddenly Matthew ceased his probing. "Let's put him back in the water, Dad, so he can go home." I flipped the thing and headed it seaward. Its tail waved back and forth as it crawled over the rocks and disappeared into the depths.

A little while later in the house, I went into the living room, and there was Maggie on the floor, her legs and arms in the air, wiggling her toes and fingers. "Look, I ho'shoe crab," she proudly exclaimed. "See me wiggle, I can't turn over. Help me." I went over to her and turned her over on her hands and knees, and with a giggle she scuttled off behind a chair.

While some psychologists think that parental nuance cues the child, I think it's just the reverse. Parents act in response to their children. Matthew's curiosity about how things work does not limit itself, for example, to horseshoe crabs and the mechanics of toys; what makes people tick is of great importance to him, too. He constantly asks such astute questions as where does blood go after the heart pumps it; how do colds get into people; why can a limb bend and why do boys have penises and girls vaginas. We encourage these questions and provide detailed answers, smiling to ourselves and wondering if this is the beginning of a medical career that will enable Matthew to support us in old age.

And while we discourage Maggie's reluctance to get her hands dirty, how can we do anything but encourage her delight in making people happy? So we laugh when she dances and, liking our appreciation, she dances more. We compliment her when she shares a toy with her brother, and by so doing, her behavior receives a little push toward becoming part of her personality.

My own childhood makes me conscious of the need for encouragement. My mother and father lived for forty-five years in a traditional marriage that, to a large extent, consisted of submissiveness on the part of my mother and bold domination by my father. I saw dependence but never love between them. I witnessed ferocious arguments, my mother's tears, my father's quiet but temporary guilt. I often wondered why they ever got married. The only reasons that I have been able to come up with are, one, they had both been through unhappy previous marriages, which they perhaps thought they could recover from by remarriage; two, my mother believed that my father, with his overbearing manner, must be very much like her own father, a figure whom she adored; and three, my father, deeply wounded by his first marriage, saw in my mother a kind smile and warm embrace.

My mother was a person of very simple soul. She loved beauty and honesty and until her last years had an unerring sense of style and an ability to discern right from wrong in their most subtle senses. But she had little sense of self. She had been an accomplished opera singer during her younger years, but my father, rather than encouraging her when he was courting her, told her that he did not like opera. She stopped singing. She stopped playing the piano, too. Over time, she stopped doing almost anything for herself. She gave over her daily life to attending to her husband and children, seeming to derive pleasure from making life easier for them. Yet I remember her talking about her love of music and her singing in a soft and thoughtful voice that made me realize that they were very important to her. I sensed that something crucial was missing from her life. When I pressed her about it, she told me that she had been raised never to think about herself and always to do for others, a common Christian dictum that most people pay superficial heed to. My mother took it literally.

My mother and father once came home from a party. He was happy and exuberant. She was very quiet. Later, I went into the darkened music room of our house, so called because my mother's baby grand piano was there, though not a note was ever played on it. But there was a record player, and it was playing Mozart. Quiet sobs came from the sofa. I asked my mother what was wrong. Between sobs, she murmured, "Nothing really; it just seems like such a waste." I am not certain what "it" referred to, but I suspect she was thinking that she had wasted a good part of her life.

I have often thought that my father would have been more content if he had married someone who better stood her ground. An entirely practical man, my father had little use for the niceties of life, save dancing. He loved to dance. But the only books he read were about sailing; he cared nothing about art or music. His favorite meal was corned beef hash with a poached egg on top, food my mother could barely stomach. He would have been happy eating nothing else.

During most of the year, he was a dirt farmer with a herd of dairy cows on a small acreage in western Massachusetts. But for one month each year, he doffed his manure-stained overalls and repossessed the casualness of his youth on Weenaumet.

My mother fit into neither of his worlds. Though she loved the rolling meadows of the farm, she disliked the grit and grime of farming. Instead, she preferred to stroll through the waving orchard grass and point out the different wildflowers to her children. My father scoffed at such impracticality. To him, the land was only for cows or for crops. Wildflowers interfered with its efficient utilization.

On Weenaumet, she was literally a fish out of water. That she knew nothing about boats and had little instinct for learning about them was her greatest undoing. My father tried to teach her, but he regarded sailing with the same stare that he gave to his meadows: one was supposed to sail not for the amusement of it, but as a means to life itself. One afternoon, the two of them set out in the Herreschoff for a lesson. I can see the scene: My mother was at the helm, nervously searching the mainsail for a sign of a luff, her hand jerking the tiller back and forth in hopes that she could avoid one. My father was sitting midship to leeward. A smile may have played over his face as he watched her, the same smile that he wears in the photograph on the mantel, a lurking smile. But today, my mother was not luffing the sail. She was tacking instead of jibing and she was not hauling the sail in when she should have been letting it out. It gave my father hope. The day was hot and bright, and the wind gentle. My father casually stood up and dove overboard, leaving my mother to her own apparently developing nautical instincts. When his head broke water, his smile had turned to a hopeful grin and he shouted to my mother to sail the boat back to her mooring alone. My mother panicked. All the security she felt in a boat was twenty-five yards away in the water. She tried to tack around to get closer to my father, but she jibed instead. When the boom swung around it hit her in the head, and she let go of the mainsheet. The boat immediately lost its heel and began to come up into the wind, sails flapping like fast drumbeats. The commotion attracted people on the beach, and they halted their conversations about sailing and boats and racing to gaze out into the harbor. My mother arose from the bilge unhurt, but her face was awash in tears. My father, probably already feeling guilt and confusion that his effort to at last make my mother into a sailor had backfired, swam to the boat and climbed aboard.

I never saw my mother at ease on a boat. She approached boats as one would a pet wolf. She often mentioned that afternoon with a laugh, as if to say that after so many years it was silly to keep thinking of it. Actually, she was haunted by the thought of ever again having to take a tiller in hand, but instead of blaming my father for his harsh teaching methods, she blamed herself for never enjoying sailing.

There is an elderly woman who lives here alone in a huge house with a roof that is an aerie of pitched cul-de-sacs and angular troughs. She and my father, as children, used to play there. One day he asked her to crew during a race. The howling wind sent waves crashing over the combing. My father ordered the girl to bail. She bailed and bailed and bailed, leaning down into the bilge to fill a bucket with water, hefting it up to throw the contents to leeward and then down again to repeat the process. Soon she pleaded exhaustion, but he told her that there was no time for that and to keep bailing. He said nothing more; the woman bailed and he sailed. After what seemed like hours, he suddenly said, "You can stop bailing now."

"What happened?" she asked, thinking that the race had been called off because of the increasing wind.

"We won," he replied. To my father, that was the essence of sailing.

My mother's failure to learn did not force a change in my father's teaching methods. He never jumped overboard with me, but I continually felt his eyes bore into me as I wondered which way I should move the tiller. He expected me to sail my first race as if I had been doing it all of my life. Instead, I ran along the starting line on the starboard tack in the middle of the fleet. Paying no heed to the desire to win, only to pleasing my father, I saw a hole to windward into which I thought I could tack and break free from the other boats. Feeling a surge of brilliant independence, I tacked, and when the sails filled, I discovered that the prow of our boat was about to cut a neighboring boat in half. I don't know whether my father's angry screams or the thud of the collision was louder. The scolding was merciless, and I was glad for the cold spray that hit my face and hid my tears. This incident is one among a flow that continued from summer to summer. I made a fool of myself coming up to moorings and docks, overshooting the former and crashing into the latter. He yelled at me and made me come around again and again, and the further off the mark I was, the louder his yells. I found myself at times so scared of doing something wrong that paralysis set in: The tiller would not move.

Looking back, I realize his struggle to teach me to sail was touching as well as cruel. He wanted only to share with his son the rather peculiar joy he found in it. He wanted his son to be as good as he. But a child does not, of course, understand such motivation. Eventually, I did learn to sail; perhaps my youth allowed me to bounce back from his tongue lashings faster than my mother could. Nevertheless, though I can sail a Herreschoff as well as anyone, I approach boats with caution, half-wondering if my father's ghost might jerk the tiller from my hand and send the craft on a wayward course toward the rocks.

August 12

During moments of anger at the children, I catch myself sounding like my father. My voice rises. I bark out commands. I must be obeyed or I will explode into a frenzy of abuse. This happens mostly when I am nervous or under pressure. At these times, I better understand the pressure my father must have put himself under during much of his life.

Both children become very quiet, too quiet. Matthew stares at the floor, his eyes frozen. The realization of what I am doing is like awakening from a bad dream in which I have turned into my father and Matthew, into me when I was a boy. I grow panicky at the thought of what I might be doing to them.

Matthew is a procrastinator. This morning we hear the thump of his feet hitting the floor and their padding sound as he comes into our bedroom and around to my side of the bed. I feel a nuzzle and a hand patting my head. I pretend to be asleep just to see what will happen next.

"Daddy"—I hear a whisper in my ear—"it's daytime. Do you want me to read you a book?" I open an eye and see Matthew staring at me. He holds the book open, ready to begin. It's one of his favorites, about a caboose that felt sad that it was always the last car until one day when the engine was climbing a steep mountain and began slipping back, the caboose put on its brakes and saved the entire train. He begins reading, not really, but he knows the words almost by heart and makes few mistakes.

I congratulate him when he finishes and tell him to get dressed quickly, we have to go shopping and get back in time for the scavenger hunt on the beach that afternoon. He asks what a scavenger hunt is, and after I tell him, he says, "Oh, that sounds like fun," and scampers to his room. Five minutes later he is lying on his bed, still in pajamas. He is on his back with legs crossed, the calf of one leg resting on the knee of the other. His mouth is pursed in a whistle, and a finger of each hand is making circles in the air. His eyes dance. I want to ask him what happy thoughts are going through his head. Instead, I sternly tell him to get into his clothes.

Ten minutes later he is still in pajamas. I raise my voice and inform him that if he does not get dressed instantly, we will go without him and leave him alone in the house—a ridiculous and hollow threat, I know, and I feel lousy making it. Willa tells him that he will not be allowed to join the scavenger hunt. Another ten minutes goes by. Maggie, dressed by Willa, is eating her Cheerios. "Where's Matt'ew?" she innocently asks. It prompts me to go into his room again. Now with his underpants and one sock on, he is lying on his stomach with his head and shoulders hanging over the bed. He is drawing something on the floor with his finger, smiling at his creation. I suppose some people would say that he is trying to tell us something and would advise us to try to coax out the reason for his procrastination. I rather think it's the age and a lively but undisciplined mind swimming in delightful awareness of a newly perceived world. For an instant I feel jealous of Matthew's abandon, of the extraordinary security that must be a part of a comfortable childhood where needs are so taken care of.

Then I fall into a rage. I grab Matthew's little body and turn him on his back. I can feel my brow arching and my lips snarling. "Here," I yell, shoving a T-shirt toward him. "Put this on this instant. And this and this and this." And I heap a pair of shorts, sneakers, and the remaining sock on him. "And if you are not out of this room in one minute, you are going to get a spanking."

I thrill at my release but feel a sickening nausea rise in me as I sense a lack of control. I am a hair's breadth away from picking Matthew up and dashing him to the floor. Or am I? Because I have never resorted to violence, though I have felt the urge many times, I have to assume that an inner self stops me just as it stops many parents in a similar situation. Nevertheless, the sensation of the desire for violence scares me. I think of those stories of children hurled from apartment building windows. As I struggle to regain my control, a picture of my father's snarling face, probably not too different from mine a moment ago, flits across my mind. His rages nearly stopped my heart many times.

Matthew is frozen, lying on his back. I retreat from the side of the bed, calmly telling him to finish dressing, ashamedly casting my eyes to the floor as I stumble out of the bedroom.

Such occurrences make me realize that my father continues to live within me. As pressures mount, pressures of supporting children, paying bills, and realizing that the years are passing all too fast, I wonder if my father's presence is not also growing inside me and that the two of us have become unwilling partners, taking absurd vengeance on those we love. Too many times when I feel the squeeze of stress, I don a suit of armor that makes me walk stiffly and self-consciously, construing anything that affects me unfavorably as a personal attack. In retaliation, I yank off my mask and spit out angry words. My father did the same.

The magazine article that I mentioned in the introduction touched upon my father's armor. He wore it when he was operating his dairy farm. It closed him off so much that he could not see the rolling hills, hear the springtime peepers in the brook, or breathe in the fragrance of the apple blossoms. My father's obsession was how much milk his cows were producing and whether the grass they ate was rich enough, legitimate preoccupations for a man who was trying to raise a family and pursue an occupation not known for its high income. But they were not the concerns of a small boy.

People who knew my father were surprised, particularly by my account of one savage incident. He was my childhood hero on the farm, I in his constant wake—milking cows, erecting fences, hauling hay bales from field to barn, collecting eggs from clucking hens. One day my father was cutting hay, and I, as usual was riding on the rear fender of the tractor. A high-pitched scream came from the long grass near the blade. We found a young rabbit with its four legs cleanly severed. My father said nothing, but carried the poor animal to a stone wall. The thing was in shock; it did not even try to hobble away on its stumps. My father picked up a rock and brought it down on the rabbit's head with such force that the head vanished, smashed into blood and fur. The body flip-flopped up and down like a shirt on a clothesline. Not a word from my father; not a glance at me, a ten-year-old boy as stunned into silence as the rabbit had been.

People had not known that side of my father, not through the eyes of a little boy who worshipped him. They had known him only as a competitive sailor or tennis player or as a man who liked to swap stories at parties.

He had a depth that he allowed no one to gaze into. If he had been able to appreciate his individuality, he would have been so much softer. The things that he did in his lifetime amaze me. For one, he ran away from home when he was sixteen and shipped aboard one of the last four-masted schooners plying the East Coast, carrying lumber from Savannah to New York. I once saw a tattered and yellowed photograph of the schooner that my mother had come upon while cleaning out a drawer. My father had never shown it even to her. The schooner was immense, with a bowsprit that jutted out over the waves like a pole over a waterfall. I tried to imagine my father crawling out there to change a jib or climbing up the ratlines that rose along the stays.

The photograph opened my eyes to a different father, one who had had marvelous adventures. I wanted to hear about his days on the boat. The only story he offered was an uninspired account of picking cockroaches out of the meals he was given onboard.

His father, an upright Boston banker, was shocked that his son had run away to sea. He sent one hundred dollars to Savannah and told him to come home. But my father returned the money and jumped on a freight train heading west. He picked crops beside migrant laborers until he reached Wyoming, where he stayed in one place long enough for one of his brothers to be sent to fetch him.

I wonder what scene unfolded when the family was reunited. I can see his mother, my grandmother, shaking her head in bewilderment and then giving the matter a shrug of her shoulders as if to say that her son's behavior was beyond her control. (That is the way she acted toward him on Weenaumet.) His father, my grandfather whom I never knew, must have ranted. My father never spoke a word about their relationship. But my mother did tell me this: My father had an exceptional mechanical ability. During his adolescence, he became fascinated with cars and one day brought home an old wreck to fix up. He had bought it with his own money, which he had saved for that purpose. When his father saw the thing leaking oil on the clean gravel of his driveway, he slammed his fist down on the table and told my father that no son of his was going to become an ordinary car mechanic. He ordered him to get rid of his prize that very day. My mother once asked my father to tell that story to me. He stopped dead in his tracks and then whirled upon her, a snarl scarring his face. "I never want you to bring that up again," he spat at her between clenched teeth. His past was a nightmare that he could never toss off.

He escaped again, this time to Honduras, where he got a job picking bananas for a fruit company. He must have been getting interested in photography then, for he took hundreds of photographs, which are in an old album near the fireplace. I take it down from time to time. My heart pounds with excitement at the scenes he shot—banana-laden boats plying jungle rivers, mule trains escorted by mean-looking little men menacing revolvers and rifles, steam engines chugging through jungle gashes, and river towns with muddy streets and corrugated tin-roofed buildings. If I had taken those photographs, I would have loved to have shown them to Matthew. But my father only told one story about his jungle days.

It involved a boa constrictor and an innuendo that, even when I was a small boy, made me uneasy. He told me that one night he had had to ride a mule along a jungle path. I never knew where he was going or why. But he told me that he carried a pistol in a holster around his waist, "just in case," he said. Suddenly the mule balked. My father spurred it, but the animal would not budge. He dismounted and tried to pull it. Then he realized that the animal was scared of something ahead of them. He peered along the path, and there, just visible in the moonlight coming through the heavy vegetation, an enormous boa constrictor was stretched across the path. My father held his bicep up to show me the creature's diameter, and my mouth fell open. He dared not go off the path for fear of getting lost. I asked him if he thought of shooting the snake. His answer sent tingles up and down my spine. "I thought of it," he said. "But I knew that the sound of the shot would give me away and they would come and kill me." He never told me who "they" were.

It might have been right after he told me the story that I began to have a nightmare, the same one over and over again. My father was in a tree and two men with clubs were trying to kill him. They had evidently struck him many times, for he was covered with blood. Now they were climbing the tree after him and he was nearly at the top. At last he could go no further. One of his assailants climbed out on an adjacent limb. I remember seeing him stand up and raise his club. My father's bloody face looked at him, his eyes wild with fear. The club began its descent. I screamed when it struck, and my mother came running into my room to comfort me. I don't know how many times I awakened her. Freud smiled every time.

Honduras was his last escapade. His father died of typhoid fever when he was deep in the jungle. Somehow his family found out where he was and sent a telegram that brought him home. It may have been the only news that would have brought him back, a reason for returning that he may have long looked forward to.

I never looked forward to my father's death, but when it happened, I felt no sadness. Only recently have I experienced any remorse that I never knew him better. I was in Louisiana on the January night that he was stricken by the flu and drowned in the fluid that filled his lungs on the way to the hospital in an ambulance. I imagine that he must have known what was happening; he must have felt his breathing becoming more and more restricted, have felt the gurgling in his pipes. I wonder if he struggled against the death he saw coming or whether a smile crept over his face with the knowledge that at last he would be free.

I was writing a book about the Mississippi River delta. The morning after he died, I was with a Cajun fur trapper making the rounds of his lines in a marsh that stretched from horizon to horizon. In the distance, a motorboat churned along one of the endless canals made by the oil company dredges that have reduced the vast Louisiana marsh to a rat's maze. With a white plume of spray rising astern, the boat zigzagged closer and closer until it came to a rest with its prow in the mud at our feet. Another trapper jumped out, an old man whom I had trapped with a few days earlier. I remember the sound of the plop of his feet in the mud. I knew why he had come.

I had said good-bye to my father just after the new year on a bright, cold morning outside my parent's farmhouse. The snow squeaked beneath our nervously shifting feet. There was not much to say; there never had been. I, subdued and angered by his existence, and he, confused that I had managed to break his hold and make a life for myself, stood facing each other. I felt no love, but he smiled a soft smile, the softest that I had ever seen on him, and said, "Good-bye, old man, take care of yourself. I hope you do something wonderful." Then the cold whipped across his face, leaving hard eyes staring at me. I turned away. Two thoughts entered my mind as he remained in the snow watching me disappear. One was that I might never see him again; the other, that it was time for him to die.

The old trapper looked at me squarely, took a deep breath, and then let his eyes drop to the mud at his feet. A second passed; he raised them to somewhere between my face and the mud and said, staring into the near marsh, "The state police called me on the CB radio. They told me that your daddy died last night. They wanted me to come and find you." He looked up at me, expecting, I suppose, to see tears spring from my eyes. That would happen in a Cajun family, where family ties and loyalty are second nature. My lack of tears confused both men. Their eyes went back to the mud. I asked in a calm voice if I could get a lift across the marsh to the bayou road, where I had parked my car. We roared off in silence.

After his father died, my father set himself up as a studio photographer in Boston and began building a reputation as the person to go to for formal portraits. Coolidges and Cabots, Lodges and Lowells, they all came to him for debutante, graduation, and wedding photographs. Eight-by-ten negatives of their aristocratic countenances filled half a dozen long wooden boxes that rested for years at the head of the cobweb-shrouded stairs leading to our attic. The boxes looked like small coffins, and as a boy, I was afraid of ascending those steps alone.

My father dropped his photography career as suddenly as he had begun it. He closed his studio and moved his new family to Hartford, Connecticut, where he got a job in an aircraft factory. Where he had learned anything about airplane engines, I do not know. His ability to assimilate new information was uncanny. After four or five years, he quit the airplane business as suddenly as he had closed down his photography studio. He took up dairy farming, not as a gentleman farmer but as a dirt farmer, who rose every morning at four o'clock to milk the cows. Within five years, he had assembled an enviable herd of

Guernseys, and young farmers from all over New England came to him for advice.

He was envied by others, too, especially those who felt trapped in office professions and yearned for the freedom they thought my father had enjoyed over the years. People spoke admiringly to me of the time he ran away to sea and of having the individuality to begin a farm. While my father would not have agreed, his life was one of glorious rebellion. It is too bad that he never had the self-pride to stand up on his tractor, beat his chest, and shout out to his little world of Bostonians that he was just trying to escape their judgmental gazes. But in his mind he never got away from them. In the same way that my father has never really died in me, his father lived on in him, judging him, condemning him, and forming in him a seething anger that he found shameful respite from through quick outbursts against his family.

Five minutes after *my* outburst at Matthew, he comes out of his bedroom dressed and smiling. I always wonder if I have done some horrible damage. Perhaps I have, but Matthew does not show it now. "Look what I did," he says proudly, pointing to his sneakers. "I tied my laces." It's true, but no bow knot is to be seen. The ends of the laces have been woven in and out of holes, around the tongue, through a sock, and plunged between foot and shoe. Tears spring to my eyes. I go over to him and give him a big hug and a kiss and tell him to eat his breakfast. Later in the day, though, my fear comes back.

Toward midmorning, after we have returned from shopping, Matthew begins asking about the afternoon's scavenger hunt. "What's a scabenger [sic] hunt?" "How does it work?" "Who will be there?" "What will I have to find?" As the hours pass, his questions become more worried and center upon his concern that he does not yet know how to read and therefore will not know what he is supposed to search for. When Willa and I tell him that he will be part of a team some of whose members undoubtedly know how to read, he seems to feel better.

Shortly before everyone is to gather on the beach, Matthew announces that he does not want to go on the scavenger hunt. He tells me that he wants to stay at home and play with his little railroad set, a gift from two years back. I think of myself as I was at Matthew's age and older. I see myself not entering sailfish races, not going to a community picnic, not playing in a softball game, not accepting an invitation to a birthday party—choosing not to experience anything that might expose me to the ridicule of others. I see the same fears in Matthew. Where do they come from? Was it all my father's doing? My doing?

I was just Matthew's age when I first remember feeling the sting of being laughed at. My parents had taken me with them to visit friends. The host liked to amuse himself and his guests by exploiting a child's gullibility. He asked me if I wanted to see a nickel fly. Eagerly nodding my excitement, I felt him insert the coin into my left ear and tap the top of my head three times. Something brushed the side of my head, and the man pointed toward the opposite wall of the room. "See it, see it," he shouted. "Over there by the windows."

I flung my arm outward and yelled, "There it is. I see it; I see it! It's flying!" The whole room and everything in it—furniture, drapes, and paintings—seemed to burst out in laughter, grating from the men, piercing from the women. I looked up, and everywhere open mouths were laughing down at me. I ran to my mother and buried myself in her lap, telling myself how stupid I had been. I stayed there for a long time. Later, I always remember fearing that some circumstance would again put me on center stage, where everyone would point and laugh at me.

My mother tried to comfort me by telling me a story

out of her childhood. She used to be a fat little girl, and all the neighbors laughed at her. Her parents told her to go out and play, but she knew what would happen if she did, so she crept out a back door of her house and hid around the corner all by herself for hours at a time. When she went back inside, she said that she had been playing with her little friends, and her parents told her what a good girl she was. I am not sure what the point of the story was, but I remember thinking it odd that both my mother and I suffered the same fear. And now Matthew. Three generations fearing that they will be the object of derision at such an early age. I wonder if the fear has a genetic explanation.

Perhaps so, but that does not mean that one can not fight it off. "No?" I feel myself shouting within me at Matthew's announcement. "I am not going to stand for it. I will not have you cheat yourself out of experiences because of the fear, inherited or put upon you by a selfish parent, that you will be the focus of curiosity, that every adult and child on the beach will stare at you, waiting for you to do something foolish."

But I say nothing of the kind. Instead, I tell him that Willa, Maggie, and I are going to the beach. I know that this statement will make him decide to come. I hope nothing happens during the hunt to reinforce his fears.

Twenty or so children are gathered on the beach with a sprinkling of mothers. I feel Matthew view the crowd and back off. He says that he wants to go out on the dock and look for jellyfish. While the hunt is being organized, he catches a half dozen of the blobs and tells me that he is a good "jellyfisherman."

At last the hunt is ready. A quahog shell must be found, a gull's feather, a hermit crab, three jellyfish, a flat skipping stone, a tennis ball, and a bay leaf. But where is Matthew? "Come on, Matthew," the mothers and children call from the beach. "We're waiting for you. You're on a team." The poor little guy is trapped, but it is a kind trap set with a spirit of support. Matthew responds with a look of shy pleasure and runs up to the oldest girl on his team—a twelve-year-old with a soft spot for him—and clutches her hand. He never lets go during the entire hunt, a sacrifice that may have cost this girl's team the prize but enabled a fearful little boy to burst with pride that night that he had been on "a real scabenger hunt" and that he had caught three jellyfish for his team.

August 13

The day is calm, and the bay like a mirror. It's just before noon. The southwest wind has usually sprung up by this time, but a cool front is approaching from the west and stops the wind from making its customary passage up Buzzards Bay. The few sailboats on the water hang as if suspended from a mobile. Suddenly the mirror is shattered by a school of menhaden circling right off the rocks. I grab a rod and reel and a lure and head for the water's edge, thinking that the presence of bluefish must be causing the smaller fish to be so skittish. Matthew does not understand my excitement, but he scrambles after me as fast as he can. After I've hopped to the rock farthest from shore, the school is only twenty feet from me. I see thousands of menhaden's dorsal fins cutting the water's surface like those of miniature sharks. The lure lands on the other side of the circling school, and I begin reeling it in.

By this time, Matthew has caught up with me, his little legs having manipulated themselves over the big boulders. "Dad, what are you doing? Why are you doing it so fast?" I hastily explain that little fish mean that big fish are nearby and that I hope to catch a big fish to eat for dinner. Suddenly, I feel a thunk, and the line arcs away from the school. The water roils, and the same excitement surges through me as when I bet on a horse. The outcome is unknown, but the thrill is not in predicting the winner; it is in the tension while the race is being run. I try to keep the fish near the surface, but it keeps thrusting downward with its powerful tail. Matthew stands beside me, transfixed. It occurs to me that this might be a frightening and perhaps incomprehensible battle to him. His only other exposure to this kind of struggle has been fishing for scup, or porgies as they are known in some parts, bottom fish that are best caught with handline and a hook baited with a slice of clam. When hooked, they tug on the line with jerks but easily rise to their deaths. Their panic deep in the green water is invisible. But *this* battle is visible and savage.

Eventually, I work the tiring fish into the shallows between two boulders. It thrashes ferociously in shortening spurts of energy. When it seems exhausted, I grab the wire leader and jerk the fish onto the shore. It is a ten-pound-or-so blue, its flanks glistening the color of a gun barrel, its strong mouth barbed with sharp teeth made to shred fish fry.

I feel immensely proud of myself. Fishing is a sport that I have delved into with furious abandon all my life for a few days at a time until I come to terms with the lack of excitement for hours at a time. I become bored and give up until the next summer. Only once before have I cast into the water from the rocks in front of the house and hooked a respectable fish. Now I stare in amazement at my catch. It is still flopping around, and with every twist of its tail I thrill to see its strength.

The fish is well-hooked deep in its throat. Blood flows freely from its gills and stains the rocks on which it gyrates. I realize that Matthew has said nothing. I look at him looking at the fish and I see perturbation in his eyes.

He feels my eyes on him. "Let's let him go, Dad," he says solemnly. "He's going to die."

My heart hardens. Let this fish go? Not on your life. That's dinner for half a dozen people. Besides, the fish is bleeding so badly that it would not live even if released. At the same time, I am happy that Matthew feels compassion for the creature, far more compassion, I note, than he appears to feel for the minnows he catches in his net. Nevertheless, minnows do not possess the glory of this fish. We have taught Matthew that killing is bad, especially the killing of useful and beautiful life, such as butterflies, lightning bugs, daddy longlegs, and toads. We scold him when he points a laser gun at anyone, and he seems to realize that arbitrary killing is evil. I am glad that he respects this fish. I explain that it will die a slow and painful death from its wound if we put it back in the water. Matthew nods, and I take the prize up to the house to display it proudly to members of the family. We eat it that night, stuffed and grilled. Matthew refuses to take a bite.

Later, as I tuck him into his bed, he asks, "Daddy, are there lots of bluefish in the ocean?" I answer that there are. "Will they be sad because the one that you caught won't ever come home?" I tell him that I do not think that fish love their family and friends the way we do. "Oh, I'm glad you caught the fish. It made you happy, didn't it?"

August 14

I played tennis this morning with the community's tennis guru, an elderly man who lives for the game. He used to play with my father constantly. Today he beat me, a defeat that stings because we have played every day for the past four days and I have won every match except today's. Now we are sitting sweaty and relaxed on the deck, nursing beers. Still proud of yesterday's fishing triumph, I begin relating my story by observing that I had seen a school of menhaden circling just off the shore.

He interrupts and tells me that he used to sit on the same deck with my father, who, upon seeing menhaden, would jump up and grab a rod and reel and head for the rocks. I decide not to continue my story; he has heard it before. But I am happily made aware by this news that my father and I responded to the possibility of catching a fish in the same way. It assures the presence of a bond between father and son, no matter how much debris buried and concealed it when I was young.

There are moments, I have discovered over the past few days, when I have taken pleasure in the memory of my father. Perhaps this is a sign that I am coming to terms with the way he was and how he influenced me. I would rather that my memory of him rest comfortably within me than forever chafe. My relationship with the children, particularly Matthew, is partially responsible for this feeling, one that a few years ago I would not have dreamed possible.

Weenaumet is a good place to test a reconciliation. It is impossible to escape my father here. There is the knotty pine covering the walls. There is the fireplace; he laid its bricks. He built the beds that we sleep upon and the railing bench that overhangs the deck. When I see a Herreschoff beating to windward in the bay, the figure at the helm could easily be he. And there is the flagpole. The community erected it in my father's memory near what some residents here call the yacht club but others more honestly refer to as the boathouse, a one-room shack toward the back of the beach. With all the understatement that typifies Weenaumet, the brass plaque on the pole reads: BILL HALLOWELL, 1906–1978. The flags fluttering aloft are as much a local fixture as my father was.

He died two years before Matthew was born. One day when Matthew and I were near the flagpole, I took him over to it and read him the inscription. "That's a way of reminding people about your grandfather, Matthew," I told him, "the one that you never knew." (The children's other grandfather is alive and well.)

"Oh," he responded vacantly. The equation between an unknown grandfather and a flagpole was not evidently apparent to him, but he struggled to make the connection. "Is Bill the man sailing over the fireplace?" he asked.

"Yes," I answered. "He was a good sailor."

"He taught you to sail, didn't he, Dada? He must have been a good sailor because you're a very good sailor."

Matthew is right. He did teach me to sail. He taught me all sorts of things, from sailing to tying knots to carpentry to playing tennis. He wanted me to be able to do what he did, to fit his image. He was a dull teacher, and I must have been a dismally slow student. We spent hours on the tennis court, he shooting me lazily arcing forehands that I returned, usually by lobbing them over the back fence. I was amazed that little me could send the ball that distance. A teaching routine developed: my father's forehand, my return lob out of the court, me tramping through the catbrier in search of the ball, and then the lecture. What I remember most about those discourses on the errors of scooping the racquet rather than swinging it horizontal to the court's surface are their length. He talked, he shadow-swung, he asked me to shadow-swing, he talked more, and then we tried it again. Everything would be fine for five shots and then over the back fence the ball would go again, followed by the search and then the lecture.

My heart was almost never in the game, my mind rarely on the ball. We had our priorities all mixed up. So adamant was he that I learn to play tennis that he carried teaching to the absurd. So concentrated was I on pleasing my father that I never really thought about how to swing the racquet. And so bored was I by his monologues and so in pain from brier-scratched shins that I ached to get off the court. I cherished rainy mornings, when I knew that the lesson would be canceled.

I learned to play, though, thanks to my father. But there are more effective ways to teach. Matthew has just begun tennis. He bats at the ball with all his might, and when he sends it over the back fence, I cheer and tell him to try to do it again. And when he hits the ball into the back court near the baseline, I like to jump over the net and give him a hug. He loves learning the game, and most mornings he begs me to play with him.

*   *   *

Above all else that I learned from my father was down-on-the-farm common sense. I value that gift highly and like to think that it was my father who gave it to me. When I was a boy, we would sometimes figure out problems together—how to build a birdhouse, to stack hay bales on a truck so that the load would not tumble off, how to plant a garden so that the taller plants would not prevent the sun from reaching the shorter ones—simple concepts that started a boy's mind thinking in terms of self-reliance. I enjoyed those times of shared ideas, though they were limited; they are the only ones I remember when my father seemed to listen to what I was saying rather than listening for what he wanted me to say.

August 15

Waves smash into the rocks in front of the house. The churned and rain-streaked water on the bay is a brown-gray. The rain is so heavy that at times we cannot see the shore. It looks as though it is going to keep up all day, one of those dreary Cape days when pitch-filled logs sputter in fireplaces, children curl up on damp couches and play quiet games, and adults resume half-read books or make lazy conversation.

Matthew and Maggie, though, want to go outside. We say no. They whine. Finally, we negotiate a compromise—they are permitted to go on the deck, even though rain spatters upon it. Maggie wants to be pushed on the porch swing. She is still in her fickle mood, on the edge of a despair into which she falls whenever her two-year-plus mind cannot understand the inevitable jostling and confusion that surrounds her. I am weary of her mood swings, from angelic laughter to tears in a split second.

I place her on the wide swing, and she sits there in a tiny pouting heap in her too-big yellow slicker, her enormous eyes staring sorrowfully from within the darkened opening of the hood. I stand in front of the swing to push it and decide to jar her out of her misery by tickling her bare feet as the swing moves forward. She looks up at me, her lower lip jutting out in a woeful curl. I keep staring at her with a big smile on my face. Finally, she relents and smiles a toothy grin of little teeth. But when I tickle her feet again, she screams, "Daddy; you push me; you no tickle."

In the afternoon, the rain still beating down, I take Matthew to see the movie *E.T.* Whenever we go anywhere in a car, he tends to work himself into a bundle of worried excitement. He seems to be a worrier by nature. That pleases me in one way; it means that he mulls things over rather than accepting them at face value. When he was two, Willa and I took him to the south of France. During the fourteen hour trip from Paris, he kept calling out our names in a singsong way to make sure we were really there.

The trip went something like this: "Mommy?"

"Yes, Matthew," Willa would say.

"You dere?"

"Yes, Matthew."

"Oh." And there would be two minutes of silence. "Daddy?"

"Yes, Matthew."

"You dere?"

"Yes, Matthew."

"Oh."

I am a worrier too, and a car trip often brings out everything I can muster up to worry about. I remember members of my family commenting upon how my grandmother worried herself into depressions in which she remained for weeks at the prospect of a trip. My father had the same tendency, especially during the winter. My car moods are more like an adult version of Maggie's everyday moods; I need a big trip with miles ahead of me to get the worrying pendulum started, and then I oscillate steadily between fair and foul humor.

Matthew's worrying in cars now comes out in the form of endless questions, many of them beginning to sound silly after the third or fourth repetition. They are not really silly at all, just an effort by a four-and-a-half-year-old to give structure to a world that is dictated to him. In New York lately, his questions have concerned what supports the streets. Rock, gravel, and sand, we have told him. He thinks about this for a moment or two before invariably asking, "But what's under *that*?" as if he is trying to get at the world's foundation. The reason for his persistence finally dawned on us, making us feel foolish. A section of street near our house had caved in, leaving a gaping hole. Matthew was fascinated by it and insisted on peering down into the blackness whenever we went near the place. His questioning was well grounded in intelligent curiosity.

Trains are another way he has devised of giving structure to his world. While cars and trucks have held him for a while, trains have long gripped him by the heart. He is on the alert for trains wherever he goes, though in New York, subways do very nicely. The sight of train tracks used to be cause for him to demand a train. "Daddy, I want to see a train. Put a train on those tracks." It was only last year that he assumed that I held the power to summon them. Now he holds the power. He exerts sole control over his own rail transportation system—his wooden train set. Their rails weave under tables and through chair legs and arch over what Matthew likes to pretend are oceans, actually stretches of floor between rugs. He can create instant towns along his routes, catapult his trains into horrible wrecks, or race them at "five hundred" miles per hour. His concentration is so intense as he builds his systems that the street outside could fall right through the planet and he would not know the difference. Standing over the realms he creates, he surveys what must seem to him to be all the track in the world, a world that he can understand. With a flick of his hand, he can direct a train to any destination of his choosing.

The real world, he is beginning to sense, is far beyond such manipulation. On the road to the theater where *E.T.* is playing, Matthew blitzes me with questions about the railroad tracks we have just passed over. "Dada, why are some choo-choo tracks so shiny and others are kind of brown on top?" "Where does that railroad track start?" "How come there is only one track here?"

To the last question, I tell him that there really is not a great demand for trains around here. "Well, if there is only one track, how do people go back to where they started?" I naively answer that they take another train back. "But how can they if there is only one track? Daddy, how many engines go on that track? Daddy, do trains here ever have accidents?" Suddenly, I realize what is going on. Next week Matthew is going to take the train from Buzzards Bay to Hyannis, one of the ventures we have planned to pay homage to his adoration of trains. He already knows a great deal about the trip. He has seen the train, the bridge that it crosses over the Cape Cod Canal, and many of the roads that it runs parallel to on the way to Hyannis. But he is evidently worried that because there in only one track, the train to Hyannis will surely collide with the train en route to Buzzards Bay. Even after I assure him that there is only one train and probably only one engine on all of Cape Cod, I can sense him churning the matter over. He ends his thinking about the problem with an alarmingly fatalistic note: "We'll see, Dad; we'll see if there's just one train on the track when we go to Hyannis."

He has been talking about *E.T.* for months. He has learned all he knows about him from his schoolmates. "But he knows exactly what E.T. does and says," his teacher gasped. I nodded proudly, once again fully appreciative of Matthew's ability to assimilate information. He regards E.T. as Stephen Spielberg designed him to be regarded by children—as a lovable creature as scared of being abandoned as any boy or girl.

Knowing that Matthew's imagination can get the better of him, I had expected him to be scared during the early scene when the children find E.T. in the shed in back of their house or toward the end of the film when the house is draped in plastic and overrun by helmeted scientists. But no. Those scenes excited him. E.T.'s drunken state, though, scared him. He did not understand the running into chairs and dressing up in women's clothes. The irrationality made him cry out right in the theater, "Daddy, why is everyone laughing. E.T. is acting just like a crazy person in New York."

Matthew's new image of a besotted E.T. lasted about one week. It pricked his mind immediately before he went to bed each night and reduced him to quaking sobs of "E.T. scares me; he didn't act right. Why did he knock things over; I don't like him."

August 16

Willa is leaving tomorrow to return to New York for a photography assignment, an interruption in our vacation that we had taken care not to think about. She will be gone for five days. I will miss her but look forward to the time alone with the kids, though its promised intensity means exhaustion. One of its challenges lies in discovering what it is like to be in a position that many women but few men find themselves in—raising children alone. Something is missing in all the talk about the new fatherhood; when it comes to doing the dirty work, many shrink back into their caves of masculine darkness, where emotions simmer and get lazy.

A friend of mine, a devoted father of two, disappears with admirable grace at the approach of a crisis. I marvel both at his timing and at his wife's tolerance of such behavior. He has honed his sense of his family's dynamics to a ready sharpness. By the noises brewing around him, he can predict when one child or another is about to throw a tantrum, has to be taken to the toilet, have a nose blown. Suddenly he's gone, seemingly vanished into thin air, to reappear in ten or fifteen minutes with an entrance that washes away the sin of his well-timed disappearance. In excited voice, he will announce that he has just worked out an incredible deal over the phone with a client. That's for his wife. For his children, he might rattle off something he heard about radio beeps from outer space being sent by life from another planet. The news he brings delights without fail.

He loves to do things with his children, this man, but they must be sufficiently diverting to distract him from the inevitable whines of restlessness that overcome children during slower-paced events, such as ferry rides or museum visits. The fact is, though, that he often proposes such expeditions. The children get excited, and his wife makes the peanut butter and jelly sandwiches. In the moments before departure, my friend begins fidgeting and throws out a few casual hints about what he really should be doing. And then when coats are being donned and the kids are peeing, so revved up about the experience they are about to have that the absence of one parent will hardly be noticed, the announcement is made with pretensions of guilt: "You know, I really promised Thomas that I would visit him, and this is the last chance I'll get. Why don't you go ahead with the children and I'll meet you outside the museum in two hours?"

My friend's wife is a kind and gracious person who generally sides with feminists. When her husband announces a sudden departure, she looks at him resignedly, a silent acknowledgment that his inability to suffer the frustrations of child rearing is a male fault of biological heritage, on a par with a man's inability to nurse.

Even women who come down hard on the side of feminist causes often separate feminism from motherhood. When it comes to mothering, these mothers are awfully soft on their husbands, who take advantage of the situation by becoming spoiled and selfish. Wives sometimes turn resentful and hard in response.

Then there are some women who do not even give their husbands a chance to be independent fathers. There are some women so efficient at changing diapers, dressing squirming children, cooking meals, washing faces and hands, and calming nightmares that they will not let their husbands dirty their hands. Or they order their husbands about as if they were nannies.

I have another friend. He comes home from work at six each evening looking forward to playing with his one-year-old daughter. When the child dirties her diapers, an agitated and confused look comes over the father's face, but he tries to ignore the smell. When his wife gets a whiff, she orders her husband to fetch a new diaper and tissues and then stands over him while he makes the change. As the evening wears on, she tells him when to get the child into pajamas, which pajamas she should wear, when she should be put to bed, and even what book she should be read.

Now, I do not speak from a pedestal. I am less adept at and less desirous of escaping the details of child rearing than is my first friend, but I sympathize with his inclination and admire his art. When clothes must be bought for the children, I beg off. When they must be dressed, I will happily do it, but I can seldom find the right things for them to wear. Willa says it's because I don't look. I ask her where Matthew's green sweater is or Maggie's red overalls. "Right where they always are; why don't you look?" comes the reply, the same response she gave me yesterday and the day before that.

I also tend to leave the children's social life to Willa, a traditional feminine strength and masculine weakness. Willa consequently spends a fair amount of her spare time on the telephone arranging play dates and pickup times with other mothers. Since I've never delved into this aspect of parenting, the thought of having to do so scares me. Willa occasionally attempts to broaden my experience at fatherhood by asking if I would make a play date for one of the children. I am amazed by and ashamed of how imaginative I suddenly become in my excuses, most of which relate to professional commitments, planned or suddenly conceived on the spot.

But I love to go off on expeditions with the children, even slow-paced ones. I enjoy cooking meals for them, giving them baths, reading to them, and putting them to bed. I have wondered why I like to do these things that some fathers consider to be women's work at worst and too mundane for their tastes at best. The reason that always comes to mind is that I never had much fun as a child. I never felt that I was pure child. Now is my chance, and I have fun being a kid with my kids, seeing the joy spread over Matthew's face when he gets on a merry-go-round, watching Maggie race around the house in her waddle, yelling at the top of her lungs her mysteriously acquired running chant: "Piggy race, piggy race, I on piggy race, Run, run, run piggy."

August 17

This morning we drive Willa to the bus station. The children are confused. Matthew knows intellectually that his mother is going to New York to "make pictures with her camera," but he feels that he is being abandoned. He keeps asking her whether she is coming back. No amount of reassurance will stop the repetition of the question. Maggie just knows that Willa is going somewhere.

After she has boarded the huge, shiny red Bonanza bus, we look up at the darkened windows in hopes of seeing her. We see nothing until a hand plasters itself against the inside of the window. The children assume that it is Willa's and begin waving with sad little motions of their arms, as if that shiny cliff of metal and glass were going to sweep away their mother forever. The three of us feel like midgets.

On the way out of the bus station, Matthew spies a model Bonanza bus on a shelf and asks if he can have it. He is so subdued in his request that I readily buy it for him. Then I drag the children into an antique store/flea market next door to scout around. Maggie is standing in front of me as I survey a pair of Windsor chairs, and I become conscious of a stain spreading on the carpet around her feet. She has peed in her shorts. "Oh Lord," think I, "what do I do now?" Willa undoubtedly would have known what to do. Mothers can handle these situations. She would have gone up to the manager and explained— a little accident, my daughter is just out of diapers, do you have any paper towels, the child is only two, smiles and apologies. But I look around and quickly rejoice in seeing that the salespeople are busy elsewhere. I sweep the kids out of that store so fast that Matthew can only gasp, "But, Daddy, you didn't even ask how much anything costs." As the door closes behind us, I notice that the stain has doubled in size as the fabric gobbles up the pee. I push the kids ahead of me down the street and wonder if at any second I am going to hear a yell behind me and the sound of running feet coming closer.

Back at the house, Matthew spends the next two hours running the model of his "Bizana" bus, as he calls it, along the deck railing. He tells me that he is "taking Mommy to New York and bringing her back." Maggie clings to me with worrying tenacity, perhaps fearing that her little world no longer exists. I am alarmed that I feel so on edge; it throws into question my self-confidence at being on an equal parental footing with Willa. I am suddenly not sure that I have been honest with myself.

Then I tell myself that this edginess is absurd. Willa will be gone for only five days, and being with the kids alone here is not exactly like being with them alone in New York. Here paradise, after all, is just outside the door.

Nevertheless, relief spreads through me when the kids begin playing together, their laughter bubbling from a bedroom as they bounce on a mattress. Though the mattress is on the floor, the possibility of disaster flits through my mind with greater ease in Willa's absence. Bumped heads and flowing tears were routine yesterday. The chance of serious injury was far more remote, and if one had occurred, we would have taken care of it together. Today, even the tears from a bruised shin would be more difficult to handle. I listen for the thud of a head on the floor and think about the thick silence before the screaming begins. The thought of concussions bothers me. If a child suddenly grows sleepy after hitting his head, he should be kept awake. But what is one to do, I ask myself, if the hurt child goes to sleep no matter how abundantly the ice is applied or how cheerfully enticements of ice cream are made? And what would happen if a disaster were to occur in the middle of the night, if a child had to be taken to the hospital? Would I have time to call someone to come over and baby-sit for the well child? Or should I awaken the sleeping child and we all go to the hospital together?

I am working myself into a frenzy, but I know it would be unfair to stop their play. The laughter is rising like gingerbread.

When I think of the children getting hurt, Maggie comes to mind. So small and so ridiculous with her waddle, she seems more vulnerable. I run through what I would do if Maggie fell asleep after knocking her head or if she cut herself so that blood poured from the wound or if she began choking on a swallowed ball. I pounce on choking as the most feared of all the possibilities. I envision her panicked and bulging eyes, her face turning red, then purple, the bulge in her throat, the flailing arms. I feel my pulse rising and shake the horrible final thought from my mind.

The growing image of death has all but receded when I become conscious of the screaming from the bedroom. Chastising myself for my foolish reverie, I rush toward the shrieks but realize by their tenor that no physical disaster has befallen the children. The problem, of enormous importance to them but only an irritation to me and one I have dealt with many times before, is that Matthew is jumping where Maggie wants to bounce. The commotion excites Brio, who commences to nip playfully at everything she can reach.

Vaguely aware that my new status as a single parent may threaten my control of the children, I overreact to the racket and order the children either to leave the bedroom or to learn to play together. They fall discomfortingly quiet, and a sad look comes into their eyes. I feel anger rising against myself for exploding so needlessly. My father jumps into my mind; he would have acted just as I did. I wonder again if I have done any permanent damage.

Their recovery from my lashing amazes me, making me feel that these children must possess an instinctual awareness of the human weaknesses that bring forth unwarranted outbursts of anger. From the mattress, Maggie lifts her big eyes and asks me to get out her plastic kitchen set that the children's grandparents gave her. She has not played with the plates and utensils in weeks, but now she begins setting the table. I wonder if such an age-old female activity is so deeply ingrained that even little girls turn to it as a way of pacifying grouchy males. She is proud of her work. At some settings she has placed two spoons beside a plate, at others, a knife and a fork beside a bowl. At the completion of each setting, she turns to me and exclaims, "Look; look, see."

Somber-faced, Matthew emerges from the bedroom to investigate what is going on. As he watches his sister, a grin that makes my heart melt lights his face. With his eyes squinting humor and his lips arching up, he appears to have three smiles. When he turns his face at a certain angle, it is lit with the gentlest rapture I have ever seen. I am amazed at how children are transformed by mood changes. Then he bursts into delighted action.

"Let's make Daddy lunch," he suggests to Maggie.

"Okay, let's do dat, lunch, Daddy," she responds with a big toothy grin. "We make lunch, Daddy."

And the two of them are off while I just sit back with a grin on my face that nothing could take off.

Matthew decides that actually I am to be served breakfast and that the menu will consist of soup, eggs, and coffee. "Okay, Maggie, let's start cooking."

"Look, we cooking," she parrots.

"We need water," Matthew exclaims. I sense a mess brewing but can do nothing to stop it. The plates and cups disappear into the bathroom, where water and giggles splash out the door. Soon the cooks come back, every container available filled to the brim and sloshing on the floor. The tablecloth gets soaked, the chairs splattered, and the meal is announced. We sit down amid the flood and begin our breakfast of "water soup," "water eggs," and "water coffee," as Matthew calls the dishes they have prepared.

August 18

The day begins wonderfully but too early. At six, I am awakened by a nuzzling on my cheek. It feels different from Brio's nuzzling, and I open my eyes to see Maggie's smiling face. "I kiss you," she announces solemnly. "Hey, where's Mommy?" When I tell her that Willa is still in New York, she nods her head in an adult way and motions to the book she is carrying. "You will read me book." Charmed, I haul her into bed beside me. The book is about a little girl who is learning to use a potty. It is explicit, showing all the appropriate holes. Maggie points to one and says, "Girls have no penis."

"That's right, Maggie," I answer, wondering if it is really possible that she chose this book as a way of acknowledging Willa's departure. "What do girls have?"

"Ah, ah," she thinks aloud, " 'gina. Girls have 'gina. I have 'gina. You have 'gina?"

"No, Maggie. I have a penis."

"Dat's right, penis." she affirms. Willa and I have never made any effort to cover our nudity in front of the children. We accept their stares and answer their questions in a straightforward way, and they treat the anatomical differences between male and female with equanimity. Curiosity is one thing, healthy by and large; obsession is quite another. My parents were considerably more nervous about their nudity than we are. They flung themselves behind a closet door or quickly draped a towel around them if they heard my approach when they were undressed. Consequently, I always used to sneak up on them and catch them in the nude, fascinated to see the differences. My interest made them nervous, and that only increased my fascination.

Despite Maggie's calm observation that she has a " 'gina" and I a penis, I feel that I want to continue reading rather than dwell on the subject. Willa and I are both struck by Maggie's flirtatious nature, not toward adults in general, which is Matthew's manner, but toward men, especially younger men. She is a beautiful little girl who knows exactly when to bat her huge eyes to best effect; she likes to choose her own clothing; she wants her hair done in a certain way. All this at two and a half.

There is a lot of truth in the old adage that fathers and daughters have a special relationship. While I have a special place in my heart for Maggie, a large reason for that has to do with her apparent devotion to me. Much of that attraction, to give Freud his due, is sexual on the part of little girls, albeit not consciously sexual. Who knows what they feel or think, really? Maybe they are attracted by the way daddys feel to their touch or the way daddys grasp them or the pitch of their voice. At this stage in her life, Maggie definitely prefers me to Willa. When I am near her, I am called to attend to her every need, whether opening a box of toys or taking her to the toilet. Her most frequent cry is "I wan' my daddy."

Right now, I think that she would be content to spend the entire day snuggling against me as I read to her in bed about this little girl who by now in the story has realized what a potty is for but keeps missing the opening.

But such wishes are not to be; her big brother, perhaps awakened by the sound of my voice discussing pee-pees and poo-poos, comes padding in holding aloft the book that *he* wants read to *him*. It's about Madeleine, the little girl in the Parisian boarding school, and her adventures with some Gypsies. It's full of dashing life and suspense.

Maggie falls silent as Matthew crawls into bed with us but starts fretting as soon as I begin reading his book. She registers most of her growing list of complaints against him—Matthew is leaning against her; Matthew is holding the book so that she cannot see it; Matthew's feet are sticking into her. Matthew raises his defense amd informs Maggie that this is *his* book and that he can hold it any way he wishes and that she can just move over if she is bothered by his leg. I fast realize that in the competition for my favors I have been forgotten. A warning bell also goes off in my head; as happens to so many parents, my children are trying to pull me apart and I'd better take a stand. A quick review of the events leading up to the present conflict tell me that Maggie is at fault, and I tell her that she must either quietly listen to the story or go into the living room and play by herself. She protests. Tears spring into her eyes, and accusations against Matthew flow forth. I take another approach; I become very articulate, a method I have found works to great effect, and tell her that I have read one book to her and that now it is Matthew's turn, that she is being a bad girl, and that I will not read any more books to her if she continues this behavior. The carrot is, of course, another book if she reforms.

She nods her head in a serious way and says, "I be good girl. I get another book." Peace at last, and the three of us read book after book. Two hours later we roll out of bed, bubbling and happy.

On the beach later in the morning, the mothers survey us with concern on their faces as if they are looking for wounds they can nurse. They ask Matthew and Maggie if they miss their mother. Instead of answering, Matthew provides a detailed account of reading books and eating French toast. They nod their heads politely, but bafflement clouds their eyes. Then they turn their questions on me. "So, they haven't driven you crazy yet? Are you counting the minutes until Willa gets back?" They seem to think that it is exceptional, really, that a man can take care of his children without a woman's help. We compare notes. I tell them of the Looney Tune times during breakfast and dinner when demands and screams fly thick, and they nod their heads knowingly. I tell them of the lovely times of reading and walking on the rocks, and they furrow their brows as if what they are hearing does not make sense.

Suddenly I realize that I am being viewed as the subject of an experiment whose happy outcome not everyone wishes for. Sadness rises in me. I am being congratulated for doing a job that women have done for centuries with little thanks. But here I am, a man, on his first solo flight with his children, and I am looked upon as having extraordinary powers. I wonder how the husbands of some of these people behave with their children. It also occurs to me that my ability to maintain the well-being of my children during their mother's absence might make some of them nervous; it might threaten their self-esteem. Fortunately for these women, they do not have to worry; I am not part of a takeover by males of traditional mothering. I am just a lone father on the beach with his children. I predict that the result of the experiment will be my being regarded as a rather odd male with a quirk that allows him to attend cheerfully to the sometime drudgery of caring for children. Some women may even lose respect for me.

This evening before the children's bedtime, we take a walk to the end of the Point. It is a peaceful time of light humor and chatting observation. Away from the shore, the wind is only a murmur through the pines, bringing scents of bay and juniper berries and the sweetness of sassafras. Crickets trill their minute chirps that begin during the closing days of July and mark the second half of summer. The trilling brings melancholy—a foreshadowing of summer's end and the beginning of fall.

Matthew pokes in the pine needles to reveal the probing head of a mushroom emerging from the acidic soil. Maggie runs along the road in her waddle and flaps her arms, telling us that she is a sea gull. The pink of the dying sun shines off her skin. I grasp their hands, bursting with happiness that they are so full of ease here. Their soft hands are lovely to hold. I am tempted, but I do not want to squeeze too hard for the same reason that I do not want to stroke a rose's petal. Even the gentlest touch might mar the perfection of the surface.

We come upon a young father out for a stroll with his son, who is halfway between Matthew and Maggie in age. The father surveys me with a questioning look. He knows that I am alone with the children, a situation I feel he would not want to be in. "Still at it, huh?" he asks in a voice that hints both longing and confusion. Perhaps he is baffled by my apparent ability to tolerate what he knows from experience must be a double dose of the usual whines of childhood. "My wife sent me off with this one because she thought she might commit child abuse." The little boy laughs and flips down from his father's arm like a gymnast. He watches with pride, and I understand where that suggestion of longing came from. He works the day through, pursuing a career he is not devoted to. He glimpses his son only during quickly darkening evenings.

August 19

Forty-eight hours alone with the kids and I am frazzled. Yesterday's delightful moments have dissolved into frustrating uncertainties. I crave time for myself, to be rid of these two demons who cling to me. Single parenting is something like working for a haphazard bureaucracy. You, the parent, like a petty officer, are deceived into thinking that you have complete power. Suddenly you discover that all sorts of rules and regulations have been set up to prevent you from exerting your authority. Example. Maggie says that she is hungry, so I, the benevolent house manager, tell her that she can have some Cheerios. Matthew is watching as I pour some into her cupped hand. As she wanders off toward the living room, depositing bits and pieces of cereal on the floor as she goes, Matthew says, "No, no, Maggie. You have to eat Cheerios in the kitchen. That's the rule." He is right; that is the rule, established a long time ago. At this point it seems like generations ago. Maggie, however, does not wish to abide by this rule. At Matthew's insistence that she eat her Cheerios in the kitchen, Maggie begins screaming that she will not.

"They're mine, mine. I eat here," she yells, stamping

her foot and clenching the cereal so fiercely that it turns to Cheerio powder. Matthew winds up for a screaming match but I intervene by proclaiming my wrongdoing. I made a mistake, I tell them, both silent now; I forgot about that rule. Maggie, this one time you can eat your Cheerios in the living room, but no more. Matthew, everyone makes mistakes, but you don't have to be a tattletale.

What I really feel like doing is telling them both to just snap out of this ridiculous behavior and have them turn to me and say, "You're right, Dad, all this yelling and screaming is not getting us anywhere. Let's stop and play together."

Tomorrow my sister will be here for the day, and I count the minutes until I have an adult in the house to talk with.

Matthew was the first to awaken this morning, at six, the usual hour. An internal alarm clock seems to go off in one child or another. I had not slept well, and what sleep I did get was interrupted by an early-morning burst of puppy energy from Brio, who started flinging a rawhide bone against the echoing knotty-pine walls. Grumpiness weighed in me, and when Matthew said he wanted to get into bed with me, I curtly told him that I wanted to sleep and that if he began moving around under the covers, he would have to leave.

When Matthew has nothing on which to focus his attention, he is an incorrigible twitcher. Sure enough, after about two minutes, his legs began to jerk around. After I hissed at him through angrily gritted teeth to keep still, he was quiet, but any further rest was made impossible by the customary morning yowl from Maggie's room.

With barely a "good morning," I extracted her from her bed and dumped her into mine and clambered in between the two urchins. If guilt and self-doubt had driven off the possibility of even daydreaming, I nevertheless felt like lying there. If the kids started yammering at each other, I told them I would just get up and leave them to scream their hearts out. But they chose this time to be good. Already they know something about self-preservation. Maggie even resumed her long-dormant routine of pointing things out: "Dere's da Brio; dere's da bed; dere's da window; hey, dere's da Daddy."

Matthew apparently decided just to lay low, but when I suggested that we all get up, he feigned sickness, a ploy he adopts when he is upset. It was a warning that I had gone too far with my little effort to lead my own life. Knowing that he was not really sick, I dragged an ounce of playfulness out of me and informed Matthew that he had a serious case of a disease called fingertip deprivation. Tickling was the quickest cure. A smile stretched his full lips. A fingertip touch to an armpit produced a staccato burst of laughter, and another to the nape of the neck dissolved him into a puddle of giggles.

Over breakfast, an ill will toward myself simmered within me. My only comfort was knowing that I try not to let the children witness my ill humor too often.

These thoughts churned away like swells rolling across the bay until they were replaced by an awareness that fascinated me: the grace with which I moved as I met the children's demands for more toast, more cereal, more milk, a napkin, a spoon. I discovered a pleasure in responding as efficiently as possible, all the time noticing the economy of my movements from bread box to toaster to refrigerator to silverware drawer to the kids' table to the fruit bowl to the sink. I wondered if the honing of such fluidity, a ballet of sorts, is a topic of conversation among mothers of young children and decided to inquire if we went to the beach.

Too late, I realized that I had made a mistake letting the children order me about. Chaos had taken over.

Matthew grabbed Maggie's peach. Maggie began screaming her high-pitched, horrible scream. Matthew laughed a
cruel laugh. Fury pumped in my heart. Fully aware that I
had snapped, I yelled at him and wound up to smack him
across the face, the first time ever. I felt the wind against
the palm of my hand as it traveled toward his cheek. I had
spanked but never slapped my children.

Matthew's eyes widened as contact became imminent. It was not a look of fear, or of anger, just a realization that something novel was about to happen. A vision
of a crumbling house of cards jumped into my mind along
with a voice—my own inside my head—warning me of
the fragility of the beauty of these children. My hand
stopped just short of Matthew's soft cheek, but the momentum carried through and I brushed it with my middle
finger. Confusion hazed his wide, still eyes. He stared at
me. A gentle smile (could it be an understanding smile?)
softened his lovely face with a calm light.

I turned away and rushed into another room, understanding more fully the sentiments of the wife of the man
we had met on the road last night, that she had sent him
out with their child because she feared that she might
commit child abuse.

Matthew came in and looked at me but said nothing.
Then he put his arms around my legs and hugged them
and whispered, "Daddy, I love you."

August 20

Where the talents and curiosities of children spring from is a mystery. Some show a bent for gymnastics or a telling sense of rhythm as early as three years. The ways and mechanisms of healing have gripped Matthew for the past two years. "What is sickness?" was one of his first abstract questions. Stethoscopes and tongue depressors and flashlights are the tools for ferreting out sore throats and fevers. A visit to the doctor is an adventure. When sick, he asks the doctor how many "antibugs" he has and whether their numbers are sufficient to defeat the "bugterias." An injection brings not tears but the curious question, "What does the needle see under the skin?"

Healing frayed emotions is a concern of his, also. He gravitates toward those who need cheering up. His grandmother—my mother—was one of the people he attended to. She suffered from Alzheimer's disease during Matthew's entire short life until she died last spring. He never knew her when she was not depressed and confused. "Al's disease," he called the affliction; his explanation for it was clean-cut and practical: "Her memory got lost in her head, and she can't find it, so everything she sees is for the first time, and she doesn't know why it's there." He was always eager to visit her, first in her drafty farmhouse in western Massachusetts and later in a nursing home in Connecticut. Out of the blue, he would sometimes say, "I want to see Bee Bong [his name for her] and make her feel better."

Stuffed animals and picture books were his aids for therapy. He would climb upon her lap or on her bed and explain what each animal did, how a bear growled and a rabbit hopped. Then he would "read" to her, making up stories to go along with the pictures. Her smile was child-like, and she hung on his every word. We all looked forward to seeing the two of them together; it gave us a chance to find a beauty in the rotting of my mother's mind and a reprieve from the quiet suffering we were all enduring.

She died in the nursing home very suddenly, about two weeks after our last visit. Matthew accepted the news with no outward emotion, his understanding of death practical as well as naive. "Bee Bong's no more, Daddy," he stated to me over and over again in response, I suppose, to my somber mood as I came to grips with her death. "It's very sad that she died, but she's no more."

He wondered what would happen to her, whether she would go to Heaven or Hell. I explained that she would be cremated and that many people believe, apparently as he does, that there really is no more life after death. Though Heaven did not catch Matthew's imagination, cremation and Hell did, fire uniting them both. When he saw a newspaper photograph of an Indian Sikh's body being burned on a funeral pyre, he pointed to the embers and exclaimed, "Is Bee Bong going to look like that?" He wondered about devils and how they could live in a place that is so hot. "I bet they get thirsty a lot," he observed.

We held a Quaker service for my mother. My father's family used to be practicing Quakers, his mother the last member who spoke in "thees" and "thous." As a child, I assumed that her shout against the wind on a howling summer day of "Are thee cold?" while we walked among the rocks in front of her huge haunting house was some kind of incantation to Mother West Wind. I wondered who these Quakers were. My sister and I evidently absorbed a respect for the religion's dignified simplicity; a plain service in which family and friends gathered to reminisce about my mother seemed appropriate. During it, I remarked that despite her love for the farm and her discomfort with the sea, we had decided to bury her ashes near where she often stood upon the deck scanning the bay for my father in his sailboat. We had placed my father's ashes in the water in front of the house. Now, her ashes and my father's could eternally remain in the same relationship as these two people so often had in life. The vision of her maintaining that patient vigil over the years shook me, and my voice began to quaver. I paused. Suddenly, little Matthew emerged from the listeners. He walked quickly to my side while a special hush fell over the room. His eyes smiled a kind of peace, in which I felt immediate reassurance. Grasping one of my hands, he turned to face the people. A murmur of appreciation ushered from them. Together we stood side by side, hand in hand, while I continued my thoughts in a steady voice.

After the service my sister came upon a letter tucked into a desk drawer. In it, my mother directed that her ashes be placed not on land but next to those of her husband in the water. Today my sister has come bearing the ashes in a tin container. We are going to take them out in *Song Sparrow* to put them next to our father's. Matthew and I eye the container, he curiously, me suspiciously. "Bee Bong is in there?" he asks wonderingly. "What does she look like? Open the can. I want to see." His questions may have more to do with understanding the essence of this person in life than with probing the mystery of death. He may believe that in that plain can lies the secret of why he was so fond of her. He fingers its lid, but I brush his hand away, realizing that I have no wish to view my mother's transformation. The thought of opening the can makes me squeamish. For some reason, I envision long-legged homunculi scrambling to lift themselves out.

The container is squarish, the kind that Italian cookies come in, and is plated in shiny brass. It weighs less than a pound, and I know that it will just bob away in the waves and probably end up on the rocks in front of the house. My father's ashes were in a great brass thing that weighed at least thirty pounds. It sank so fast that the water seemed to snatch it out of our hands.

The only solution, short of opening the lid and letting the demons out and the water in, is to punch holes in the sides. I take the container to the basement, with Matthew hot on my heels hoping for a peek of Bee Bong. As I hammer holes, white ash, essence of Bee Bong, seeps out. Matthew waits expectantly for something more definitive to emerge, the stuff of religion, but nothing does. He casually fingers the white stuff, blows it away, and wanders off to launch one of his spaceships on a quest for Darth Vader's *Death Star,* the mystery of life and death remaining unknown.

Bee Bong is not as willing to join her husband as her unexpected letter would have us believe. My holes are for naught; the can will not sink. As I watch it float astern of *Song Sparrow,* I am convinced that my mother would be better off on dry land. She should not have written that letter, subservient to him even after he was dead. The rolling hills of the farm would have been a far more appropriate place for her.

We tack around to retrieve the can, approach the spot where we remember we had lowered my father's

ashes over the rail, and try again to sink my mother's remains, this time by holding the vessel underwater so that
it will fill. But it bobs right back to the surface. *This* really
is the stuff of religion.

We make another attack to pick up my mother's unwilling ashes. Our last resort is to open the can and let the
water flood in. I hesitate. My sister grabs it and pries the
lid off, but I notice that she does not raise it more than a
quarter of an inch. That is enough. A stream of light
shines inward, and our eyes helplessly follow.

We see ashes and something else as well; it looks like a
miniature scroll. My fingers burn to know what is written
on it. "Look, a message, a message from Bee Bong," yells
Matthew. "Let's see what it says." My sister and I ration-
ally agree that it is probably an identification inserted by
the funeral home, giving my mother's name and date of
death. But I wonder, even though I don't want to touch it.
My sister plunges the partially opened can into the water
and holds it there before pushing the lid back on and letting go. The can drifts slowly downward, its brightness reflecting rays of sun. As full of water as it must be, its final
journey is a reluctant one. Though the water is too deep to
be able to see the bottom, I can envision where the can
will come to rest—upon a sandy ridge, swaying this way
and that as the currents churn about. It will fret as my
mother had in life, yearning to alight somewhere else but
not having the self-confidence to. Unless a hurricane's
force on the waves eventually nudges the can ashore, the
ashes will probably stay right there next to my father's,
forever restless.

August 21

The wreck of an old wooden barge is a source of constant fascination here, a cattle barge that parted its tug's towline during a storm ten years ago and smashed onto the rocks near the house. Fortunately, there were no cattle on board, but there had been recently, for hay and bits of hair were still stuck in the splintered wood.

The timbers are massive, great ten-by-ten beams and four-by-twelve planks. Men with chain saws descended upon the rocks after the accident and picked at the barge's bones, carrying off the wood to fashion it into planters and patios, though one man told me that he was going to build a bathroom with the beams. I wondered if it was to be used by a family of giants. What remains now hardly looks as though it was once part of a vessel. It's a splintery platform of rough planks held together by rusted spikes. Broken beams angle off it, hinged to the bulk by grotesquely twisted iron straps.

Whenever we walk to the beach along the rocks, we take a route that brings us to these remains. Today, Matthew climbs aboard the platform as usual and pretends that he has just been shipwrecked. Accustomed to this game, I walk to the far end of the planks and am about to jump off to continue hopping from boulder to boulder when something stops me and I wheel about and stare back in horror. Matthew has edged out on a beam from which most of the planks have been stripped. Only one four-by-twelve rests on it. Jagged rows of bent spikes jut from both sides. The beam appears detached from the wreck but is held off the ground by a huge boulder. Now clinging to the wood with his hands like a monkey on a limb, Matthew scampers over the boulder and heads for the beam's far end, suspended a few feet off the ground. My horror is that each time he moves, the plank with the iron teeth bounces toward him. The beam is a deadly see-saw, the boulder its fulcrum. So fascinated is Matthew with his newfound climbing agility that he is oblivious to the plank's movement. The farther he travels from the fulcrum, the greater the shifting, a booby trap conceived and set by fate. Just as I yell a warning, he takes a giant step. Now unbalanced, the end that he is near plunges toward the ground, and the rising plank on the other side of the fulcrum slides down the beam's top, its weight about to crush Matthew's legs and its spikes to impale him. His eyes widen and he freezes. I know that there is nothing I can do to turn the course of this disaster. I can only stare helplessly; the entire sequence of events has consumed no more than three or four seconds. Suddenly, I hear the sound of tearing wood from the plank's other end, and its momentum slows. Concealed spikes on the far end still attach it to the platform, preventing it from completing its descent. It stops two inches short of Matthew's legs.

When I reach his side, he is staring at the spikes, an uncertain look on his face as if he knows that something terrible was about to happen but is not sure of the extent of the danger. I grab him in a hug and explain what almost happened. He nods and turns to me. "It's all right, Dad. Relax. Nothing happened. But that was pretty close,

wasn't it. Dad? I almost got stabbed, didn't I?" As I
tear apart the unintentionally cruel trap, I wonder that
Matthew does not lose his composure now that he understands the physical forces involved and the weight of the
plank sliding toward him. But as we continue on our way
to the beach, all he says is, "I must be growing a lot to be
big enough to have moved that heavy board." I am still
jittery. I cannot stop touching Matthew and keep putting
my hand on one of his shoulders or patting him on the
head as if to confirm that he is still there.

I wonder if my overwrought state dates back to a
time when tragedy almost struck me when I was
Matthew's age. It was on the farm. My father was backing
a trailer attached to a tractor up to a loading ramp, and I
was foolishly hanging onto the back of the trailer, suspended off the ground. Suddenly I slipped and fell.
Everything continued as if in slow motion. I was transfixed by my own paralysis and the trailer's heavy wheels
coming toward me. I saw where one of them would strike
my outstretched leg and wondered whether it would hurt.
I was aware how pleasant the cool grass felt on my bare
arms and I remember being able to look along the bottom
of the trailer's chassis and see my father on the tractor
seat, his head turned as he looked backward.

Almost casually, he stopped the tractor. He never got
off but ordered me to get out from under the wheels. Like
Matthew, I knew that something momentous had almost
happened, but, never having experienced real pain, I had
no inkling of my good fortune that my father had noticed
me on the ground behind the trailer.

I pulled myself out from underneath, and he continued backing up to the ramp as if nothing had happened.
Confused by my father's coolness, I began to tremble and
turned away, ashamed of the tears. Reflecting upon that
time, I don't believe my father ever noticed my state, only

that I had not been physically hurt. To him, tragedy and near tragedy were far apart and not worthy of the same consideration. I had escaped unscathed, and everything was as it had been.

He treated himself similarly. When I was five or six, our bull almost killed him. His name was Lochinvar, named after the bold lover and hero of Sir Walter Scott's ballad *Marmion*. He was a huge animal with a neck that reminded me of a bulldozer's power and balls that hung nearly to the ground. I wondered if their swinging to and fro bothered him as he moved about his enclosure, sturdily bound by a high fence of oak planks. That was his outdoor home, to which he was led every morning from the barn, not by putting a halter around his head and pulling him along with a rope but by hooking an iron rod to a copper ring through his nostrils and tugging.

While the cows grazed on sweet grass in the meadows, Lochinvar wallowed in the mud of his pen. One day my father, thinking the animal was bored, gave him a toy. I was alarmed when I heard this. To me, a toy meant one of *my* toys, and I hoped with all my heart that it was not the little red jeep that I was so fond of. I ran to Lochinvar's pen, and there, to my relief, saw the animal charging a huge log that my father had attached by one end to a dead tree in the middle of the pen. Head lowered, he rammed it again and again with massive butts and caught it on the back swing with his horns to flip it off to one side like a soccer ball. He seemed to have nerves on the tips of his horns that enabled him to catch the log on his great head at just the right moment.

Lochinvar had only one function on the farm—to pass his admirable genes on to the herd and improve its milk production. He was a breeding machine, and every mating was preceded by a ritual. Each time a cow came in heat, she was tethered outside his pen. My friends and I watched the proceedings goggle-eyed from a short distance away behind a series of fences, aware that something was about to happen that would result eventually in a calf being born. It never entered our minds that people, our own parents, could engage in similar behavior. Lochinvar knew what was about to happen, though. He was raving inside his pen, pawing the mud and snorting with head lowered and eyes rolling—every show of machismo that a bull could muster.

Outside the gate, my father contributed to the animal's agony by asking such inflammatory questions as "Are you ready, Lochinvar? Are you all set, boy?" Then he would fling the gate open and stand behind it. Lochinvar would hurtle out and literally jump on the poor cow. It was all over in ten seconds. The deed transformed him into a docile beast. He would shuffle back to his pen, staring at the ground with a dazed look.

One time, the ritual did not play out so smoothly. The cow was tied and waiting. Lochinvar was pawing and snorting. We were watching at our usual station. My father flung open the gate. The bull jumped out, but instead of going for the cow, he went for my father tucked behind the open gate. Head lowered, he charged, and my father, realizing that he would be crushed between the gate and the pen, stepped free. But the bull, with the same uncanny agility that he used in his play with the log, tilted his head and caught the bottom of my father's pants on one horn. He jerked upward, and my father was four feet off the ground before the pants ripped and he fell. But a horn caught on his belt. I don't remember being stunned at what was happening. I did not feel the urge to cry out or even realize that my father was in danger of losing his life. I only remember the slow motion, the distinctness of every second, the same clarity that I had experienced when the trailer's wheel was coming toward my leg.

The bull lifted my father again, but he struggled backward and fell free to the ground. Then he screamed. It was a scream of futility, not of pain or of fear. He saw the bull charging again. Its huge head seemed to grind my father right into the dust. But he only caught his shirt with a horn. He raised his head, and again my father was lifted into the air for the third time until, like his pants, the material gave way and he fell to the ground. Lochinvar suddenly abandoned his attack. More important things compelled him. He went for the cow and mounted her. My father, unscathed, got up. His clothes fell right off his body. His face was white and his hands shook. But he did not back away from the bull. He walked unsteadily to him, put his finger in his nose ring, jerked him off the trembling cow, and led him back to the pen.

That evening, he joked about bullfighting to my ashen-faced mother. If the experience ever had an effect on him, he never let on. Such stoicism was part of his makeup.

Many years later, I came to understand that quality at a time when I thought I was about to die. It happened in the Peruvian jungle, where I was living on a college fellowship. I was walking along a path high above a roaring river. Night fell and our group still had several miles to go before reaching the camp. We had no flashlights with us, and candles were useless in the sporadic tropical downpours that made the rocks on the path treacherously slippery.

I was conscious at one moment that the path narrowed and that the river seemed right below. The next moment I slipped. The embankment was so steep that I barely touched the tree trunks and rocks that were hurtling by. A deep calmness pervaded my mind and body, though I was certain that death lay seconds away. I felt like Alice must have as she fell down the Rabbit's hole.

Suddenly, I came to a cushioned stop, caught in a moss-coated angle between a tree trunk and the embankment.

It had been an exhilarating few seconds. Contentment flowed through me that I was not going to die after all. But the shrieks I heard from above let me know that my colleagues assumed that I had already been smashed to pieces among the river rocks below. Slowly, I inched my way upward, leveraging myself from trunk to trunk until my voice could be heard above their clamor. When I arrived back on the trail, relatively unscathed, I was met with embraces and kisses and tears of joy, all of which I appreciated. But I also remember my matter-of-factness about the incident, which reminded me of my father years earlier. I fell, but nothing had happened, after all. Matthew had reacted to his near-tragedy with the same nonchalance.

August 22

Since Willa's departure, we have established a routine helped along by the weather that is typical of late August—hot, still days and chilly nights that encourage deep sleep. As soon as the kids get up, they troop into my bedroom with books under their arms. They snuggle down on each side of me for a reading. Though they each have their favorites, there is one that seems to cast a spell over both of them. It is *The Wreck of the Zephyr* by Chris Van Allsburg, a magical story about a boy who dreamed that he was on an island whose inhabitants could sail so well that they could make their boats rise out of the water and travel through the air.

The boy practiced and practiced, but his boat would not rise, until on one beautiful night he learned the skill and sailed high above the clouds back to his home. As he approached the village, full of his new discovery, he thought he would awaken and astonish the sleeping people by ringing the boat's bell. But inexplicably, the *Zephyr* began to descend, and he could not make her go up again. Soon she was on a level with the pine trees and then, with a frightful tearing sound, she ripped into the branches and fell to earth, broken and graceless.

Every morning the children insist that I read this book to them while they pore over the richly textured illustrations. The book's permanent place is here. We have taken it to New York a few times, but the kids ignore it there. We have taken it to the country on weekends. It goes unread. They must sense a parallel between the story and their perception of the Point. Both possess magic, both are far removed in temperament from the real world.

Our lives are of little rituals—of reading in bed, of eating breakfast on the deck with the sun warming our unreal world, of the kids' mania for swinging on their swings that look as though they will carry them high above the pine trees and into the ocean. While they swing, I work nearby on a tree house I am building for them. I have worked it out so that I am able to push them as high as their swings will allow and know that I have time to saw three boards before their momentum is lost and they beg for another push.

They both want to help me in my carpentry. Maggie picks up a screwdriver just as I am nailing a board in place and offers it to me, insisting that I take it then and there. "Quick, Daddy, take it," she says. "I he'p you." Matthew practices his own hammering by standing a row of nails up in a board and then pounding each one down. Then he gives me the board and tells me that it will make the tree house stronger. I do not attempt to discourage this experimentation, but I keep a watchful eye on the tools they pick up. What is most striking about now as compared with three days ago is the calmness about us. I feel that I am tougher, able to bear up under the whines rather than becoming overwhelmed by them. Perhaps this is one of the reasons the kids do not whine so much now. They realize that one parent can no longer be played off against the other. We form a tight little unit.

When we go to the beach, I unpack the car with determination, aware of but not so sensitive to the still-concerned glances of the mothers. Their interest is tempered now. I guess I have passed some kind of test, probably because I never sought them out in desperation. And it must be obvious that the children have not suffered in Willa's absence.

Proudly, I know exactly when to force a peanut butter and jelly sandwich into Maggie's hands to ward off the whiny "I hungry" already forming in her throat. I know just when Matthew has had enough swimming practice and is ready to slip into his bubble so that he can do "some real swimming," as he calls it.

The big difference between today and the previous four days is that today Willa is returning. I told the children this morning that "Mommy is coming back this afternoon." Matthew's immediate question was, "Is she going to bring me a present?" His second question was, "How long is she staying?" I am impressed by the children's adaptability; the rituals they have evolved over the past four days have left no room for another person. Like a swarm of insects, they have closed the gap left by Willa's departure and now they seem oblivious that someone was missing. Their fluidity frightens me. I have always wondered how very young children, as contrasted with adolescents, are able with such seeming ease to adjust to divorce or to the death of a parent. Now I have a better idea. Just as Matthew's young mind dealt so blithely with his near-accident on the barge yesterday, he has needed only a few days to smooth over the rough edges left by Willa's departure.

By prearrangement, Willa had told me that she would meet us on the beach to surprise the children. When she arrives, Maggie throws a fit that would have made Freud applaud himself. "I wan' my Daddy. You go

'way," she yells as Willa approaches with arms outstretched. "You go New York." Matthew is civil but distant in his greeting: "Hi, Mommy, did you take a lot of
nice pictures? You know what we're doing? We're building a tree house?" Willa looks at the other mothers. She
understands enough about kid psychology to know what is
happening, but it still unnerves her a bit. The other
women, know, too, and there is a laughing outbreak of female communication that I appreciate only intellectually.
Then Willa begins to joke that since everything seems so
nicely under control, she might as well go right back to
New York. Matthew, forever listening and watching,
whirls around. "Mommy, you're staying, aren't you?" His
voice rises in panic and he runs to Willa and launches
himself at her with a great little-boy hug.

August 23

The short-lived peace that the children and I had arrived at apparently vanished sometime last night. Grouchy children rise with the sun. Matthew wants to get into bed next to Willa. Willa wants to sleep, still exhausted from her photography job. But Matthew wants her attention; he begins twitching, making further sleep impossible. Willa grumbles.

Maggie will have none of getting into our bed *this* morning, now that her morning place has been repossessed. She goes into the living room whining, but comes back a second later howling, Brio giving her puppy nips to the heels. What can one do at this hour with two misbehaving children whose echoing yells so jar the morning calm?

Today is the day we have decided to make that train trip from Buzzards Bay to Hyannis in order to let Matthew experience a real train. I know that the first train leaves Buzzards Bay just after seven, much too early to prepare for the journey but a fine time, under the circumstances, to rush to the Cape Cod Canal and watch the lowering of the drawbridge and the train crossing it.

I excitedly tell the kids about my idea. For once,

Matthew does not endlessly dawdle while dressing. For once, Maggie does not squawk while being dressed. I quickly fill two plastic Baggies with Cheerios, and we are off. It is lonely at that time of the morning at the edge of the canal beside the bridge. Fog swirls off the fast-moving water in smoky streamers. The elaborate ironwork of the massive bridge looks cold and unfriendly. Matthew stares up at the huge span far above that in about two minutes should come groaning down to let the train pass. The track we are standing beside is covered with grease and debris. "Daddy," he whispers, "this isn't like my Brio set. I like my choo-choo better."

Maggie flaps her arms at a gull standing on a rock nearby and orders it to fly. "You fly, gull. Fly. See, watch me." And she waddles toward it, motioning with her arms. The gull, perhaps used to children's antics, cocks its head and regards her warily. But a metallic booming sound echoes from far above, and the gull shrieks in reply as the tons of iron above begin their descent along the two towers at each side of the canal. Matthew and Maggie look stricken. "Daddy, get away, get away. It's going to fall," Matthew yells and tugs at my arm.

I imagined that this was going to be his reaction. His seemingly inborn sense of safety and order has taken hold. In New York, when we are waiting for a subway together and I impatiently go to the edge of the platform to peer along the track to see if the train is coming, Matthew reproaches me with a "Daddy, you know you are supposed to wait behind the line. That's very dangerous." I respect his concern and quickly comply, thinking of news stories of someone falling or being pushed onto the tracks.

The scene before us here is far more ominous as the span with the railroad tracks comes down. It is immense, and the cables that support it look like spider's thread. Every few seconds the towers emit dull clunks and wrenched grinding sounds as metal strikes metal. Across the canal, the waiting train blares impatiently, its blinding headlight an angry scream. Matthew backs away, and I follow, grabbing Maggie, who stares uncomprehendingly at the hellish scene before her.

With a final crash, the span settles down on a level with the track, and the barrier gates go up. The huge diesel engine rumbles across the canal toward us. I am thrilled and move a few steps closer to the track. The engine is just an old battered one, scarred and scraped and with chipped paint, but its power is awesome. Matthew is not so thrilled. He cowers behind me and won't even wave to the engineer, an old man with a flowing gray mustache who looks somewhat hurt by Matthew's rebuff of his friendly greeting.

As the last car disappears around a curve and we cross the tracks to return to our car, Matthew kicks the steel and observes, "You can't change these tracks around. That's what I like about my Brio. I can make it go anywhere. Daddy, do we have to take that train to Hyannis? Let's not, 'cause we know where that train is going."

I agree. We'll save it for another time.

August 24

It's Saturday, which means there is a race this afternoon. Though I have entered numerous races since my childhood days, when my father made me miserable by badgering me around the course, a Saturday never passes now without some twinges of feeling obligated. If I do not race, I feel that I should; a moral duty has been drummed into me. If I do race, my father's voice beats to windward with me, scolding me for luffing and chastising me for not properly setting the spinnaker.

One of my secret desires is to be free of any qualms about racing or about not racing. I want not to care and the best way to do this is to try to calm my nerves when I race. So today, the wind blowing gently out of the southwest and under a sky marked with puffy clouds, I decide to race. Willa agrees to crew; a baby-sitter will take care of the kids.

Like my father only a decade ago, I am all atwitter before we leave the house. "Where's the stopwatch?" "Where's the spinnaker?" "Where are the spinnaker sheets?" "Matthew, I'm too busy to show you how to draw a whale."

Willa casts a warning eye at me as if to say, "You're

being a jerk. You sound just like your father, and look what he did to you."

Willa felt sorry for my father, but his harsh ways made her seethe. Not long after I first introduced my parents to her, she had a run in and a showdown with my father. She was taking a shower and accidentally splashed some water on the bathroom floor. My father went into a rage. He stormed up to her and snarled. "How could you have done that? I thought only children were so sloppy."

With all the freedom that lack of familial proximity provides, Willa faced him squarely. "How dare you talk to me like that? No one talks to me that way." My father's shoulders arched back as if he had been struck by a tornado. Then they slumped, and to my amazement fear crept into his eyes. He didn't say another word; he just turned around and walked out of the house. An hour later he returned, bearing a strange peace offering—a jar of grapefruit juice. Willa is addicted to grapefruit juice. She gave him a big hug and he blushed.

Despite my treatment of Matthew, he bids us good luck as we head off for the beach and the harbor. "Good luck, Daddy and Mommy," he says. "Don't tip over *Song Sparrow.*" In the harbor the regular racers banter back and forth as they ready their boats. I am jealous of their ease. It seems so alien to me to possess that confidence before a race. I am also irritated by my knowledge that though I can sail every bit as well as they, I still feel the bad memories tighten my nerves and muscles. If I let the irritation dominate me, I know I will not have a very good time during the two-hour race. My father is no longer watching me, I remind myself; I have to consciously think that, almost like literally heaving his weight off me. As we sail out of the harbor, I feel lighter and freer.

Eight or nine boats are at the starting line, and I make a graceful but conservative crossing, keeping my father sloshing around down in the bilge. Now we are alone, beating to a buoy far out in the bay, separated from the other boats by swells and opposite tacks. Though aware of the competition, I find a pleasant freedom in just sailing the boat the best I can. She springs ahead as she climbs each wave's crest and settles comfortably in the troughs before scooting ahead again.

We are fifth in place rounding the buoy but lose a boat when I mess up setting the spinnaker properly. The damn thing is upside down and caught under the bow. My father's voice rumbles, and I tell it to shut up. "I haven't set a spinnaker for three years, so get back down there under the floorboards where you belong." I finally free it and get it up the mast right side up. It begins to draw well, and we pick up the boat we lost and gain on another. At the end of the next leg I am prepared to raise the spinnaker again as soon as we round the mark. The boat surges ahead, and we become so mesmerized by its rise and fall as swells pass under her that we do not realize how much we have gained on the lead boats. Suddenly, there's the finish line. We cross it and, "oh, my God," we've come in third. A yellow flag and congratulations are waiting for us. On the sail back to the harbor, I am full of satisfaction, but not jubilance. I feel as if I had spent part of an afternoon partaking in something pleasant but not too exerting. Repeating this too often, I think I would get bored. A new sorrow for my father passes through me. He took the outcome of each race as a personal loss or triumph. The poor man never learned to laugh at the races and enjoy the movement of the boat through the water.

When we return to the house, Matthew jumps at the pennant. "Daddy, can I have it? I want to put it up over my fort so everyone will know that the pirates are at home."

August 25

We have been ignoring Maggie, and now she is letting us know about it. Second children everywhere must suffer being ignored. The gurgles and snorts of the firstborn are extraordinary for their novelty; of the secondborn, third-born, and all that follow, cute but predictable. I was the secondborn in our family, and my mother kept a journal of my first twenty-five days. Then she stopped. Her journal of my older sister continued for a number of years, complete with photographs.

I swore that I would treat my children equally. After Matthew was born, Willa and I devoutly kept a journal for one and a half years. Maggie's lasted all of three weeks.

And what a mixed blessing for a younger child to live under the shadow of an older sibling, especially if the two are close in age. Maggie is Matthew's parrot and mimic. Her attachment to him is obvious. When Matthew does a somersault on the lawn, Maggie says, "Look, I do somes'ing [sic] too," and collapses folded up in the grass. Yet, there is so much that she cannot do that Matthew can and Matthew is at an age of incredible learning. His independence, his reactions to new things, his increasingly sophisticated mental connections, are wonderful to see.

Yesterday, a favorite friend of his was supposed to come over and play but could not at the last minute because of a fever. When I told Matthew, he twisted and turned his body in unarticulated disappointment. I asked him if he was sad about it and he replied, "Yes, Daddy, I'm disappointed, but you know what, Daddy? Everyone has disappointments"—a hard-knocks-of-life philosophy we had provided him with and he was actually putting it to use. Maggie can scarcely keep up at her age. That she should not be expected to sometimes falls by the wayside.

And now she feels abandoned, though I do not think for a minute that she is aware of these feelings. Indeed, it is possible that I am only imagining that she is reacting at all. Nevertheless, her toilet-training progress has tipped my thoughts in that direction. One day when she was about two, she decided that she wanted to pee in the toilet. No potty for her, thank you. Though fearful that this was merely a temporary aberration that would quickly slide right back into Pampers, we congratulated her. Now, congratulations have become a habit. Every time she pees or does "do" we exclaim "Good girl, Maggie!" and she grins in the luxury of our praise.

But something has backfired. For the past two weeks our instantly toilet-trained Maggie has been peeing in her pants all over the place. One thought for why she chooses to do this is that in the praise we have lavished, we have inadvertently put too much pressure on her. Somewhere in that little head, she may have been striving all her waking hours for that "Good girl, Maggie." At a certain point, perhaps the struggle to control her bladder became just too much. Burned out at two and a half by proud, pushy parents.

Maybe there is another reason. She gets a lot more attention when she pees in her pants than when she pees in the toilet. Then she only gets a "Good girl, Maggie," praise which may be getting a bit perfunctory and repetitive. But the other way she gets "oohs" and "aahs" as everyone watches the puddle on the floor grow larger. There's a scramble to clean it up before it stains the wood. She gets to be taken to the bathroom and swabbed off, then to the bedroom for a change of clothing. Then she gets a few words of gentle advice to the effect that next time it would be nice if she told someone that she had to pee so she could be put on the toilet.

I think I am on to something with this theory because two new behaviors have become more common over the past three or four days. One is a horribly frustrating game that goes like this:

"Daddy, I have to go pee."

"Okay, Maggie, let's go to the toilet." We go into the bathroom and I put her on the toilet. She sits there for a minute.

"No, I don't have to."

Fifteen minutes later, "Daddy, I have to go to the toilet."

"Are you sure?" I ask and receive a sincere nod.

Onto the toilet she goes again followed by a "Daddy, I don't have to."

Pediatricians and child psychologists like to say that this behavior is a nascent sign of independence on the part of the child, who is letting parents know that even though they have to pee, they are not about to fulfill an adult's wish that they do so in the toilet. The idea, then, is that the child has a number of alternatives to choose from—peeing in the toilet, peeing on the floor, pleasing a parent, displeasing a parent. Maybe.

The other possibility has to do with "do." Yesterday, it occurred to me that Maggie had not gone in about four days, which may explain her second new behavior, one that worries me—her constant complaining of a stomachache. The poor girl; she has not had a bowel movement in four days and all she does is complain of a bellyache. I would be screaming. But the complaining gets to us. Each time, we ask her if she has to go to the toilet. We offer her apple juice, prune juice, prunes, strawberries, fruit. She shakes her head mournfully at each suggestion and looks as concerned about her problem as we do. We discuss the possibility of intestinal infection; we talk about taking her to a pediatrician. She seems to show great interest in our efforts to find the solution to her pain.

I do not think that she needs prune juice or a doctor. I think she is telling us something very important with these complaints, something that has very little to do with her intestines. She is getting a lot of mileage from our concern; the attention she is receiving is all hers. Her older brother cannot creep around the corner and steal the show. As I think about this, I see a solution to her problem and also I see the trap of family togetherness. We like to do things together, nice in theory but a sentiment that favors Matthew. He is the one who can catch jellyfish, hit a tennis ball, pretend to be able to sail a boat, swim by himself, and so on. Everyone exclaims over his feats, leaving Maggie lost and alone. It makes much more sense to do things separately with the children for a while, so that either one child can have both parents or one child and one parent can be together.

Tomorrow, I decide I will take Maggie blueberry picking—no big adventure, but something that just the two of us can do together. Willa will take Matthew off somewhere else.

August 26

I want to pick blueberries with Maggie for a couple of reasons other than for the opportunity it gives her to be alone with a parent. A feeling is in the air that summer is drawing to an end. We have not picked any blueberries, and a vacation here isn't complete without native blueberries. People here are moving faster in the knowledge that the exodus to winter quarters will begin in a week. They are prompted by the night's chill, the turning of the oaks, and the talk of children about returning to school. We'd better hurry.

There's another reason, strange sounding. I want to be sure that Maggie's first blueberry-picking venture is a fun one. The desire is spurred on by the knowledge that even something as banal as picking blueberries can sourly influence a child's memory. A person should look back on childhood blueberry picking on Weenaumet with pleasure and her mouth should begin to water for the tart but juicy berries, her nostrils should fill with the remembered scent of freshly broken bay leaves and pine needles, and her ears should hear the distant flap of sails on the bay and the rasping of cicadas in the tree tops.

I picked my first blueberries under the stern surveillance of a nanny with the clipped voice of Mary Poppins and none of the magic. Her hair was done in a massive ponytail that hung halfway down her back. She switched it about to get rid of flies. One afternoon she pressed some of my cousins and me into service. We were told to dress in long pants and long-sleeved shirts and report to the kitchen. There the nanny pointed to a large bowl and informed us that by evening it had to be full of blueberries or else. She then provided each of us with a plastic cup and marched us to a favorite blueberry patch in the middle of a forest of poison ivy. We were ordered to fill our cups and not to eat any berries along the way. I ended up with only half a cupful, for which I was soundly scolded. But worse, two days later I began squirming with the most horrible itching I have ever known. My cousins began to itch, too, and my grandmother's house was soon full of itching children who never wanted to pick blueberries again. I have thought with pleasure what the adults in the house must have said to that nanny.

I want Maggie to think back on this day and smack her lips. I tell her what we are going to do, just she and I, and her eyes light up. She waves the plastic cup I have given her and shouts, "Hey, Daddy and I going to pick strawberries. We pick strawberries. You want some?"

"No, Maggie," I correct. "We're going to pick *blue*berries."

"Yeah, we pick strawberries."

We start off for a path through the woods near the house, one that I know is bordered by full blueberry bushes that by now should be dripping with fruit. The pines nearby are tall and straight and the undergrowth broken by rotting windfalls. The path is little traveled, one whose direction must be searched out with care.

We walk along it for only a few minutes before Maggie says, "Daddy, I 'cared. Carry me."

I laugh softly and reassuringly and gently inquire what there is to be scared of.

"Dinosaurs," is the reply. And then the order: "You *will* protect me." We have heard this command a lot lately. I am touched by its comprehensiveness. Its phrasing "You *will* protect me" is the essence of Maggie right now. That she utters such a command shows the healthy birth of an independent spirit. But the message itself echoes her vulnerability in a world of imagined and real unknowns.

I tell her that there are no dinosaurs here or anywhere else. "Besides," I add and stop and kneel down to her level, "you know how to kick and pop dinosaurs. Show me how you can pop a dinosaur."

She winds up with a tiny fist and thrusts it up into the air. "See, I pop dinosaurs." Then she raises a sandaled foot and stamps it into the pine needles. "An' I kick dinosaurs."

Her fear of dinosaurs, and alligators, was more pronounced until a few weeks ago, when we took her shopping for a pair of high-top leather shoes, a miniature version of the kind that a construction worker might wear. She was immensely proud of them and wore them right out of the store. When we got back to the house, she summoned us to her bedroom and informed us, "Now, I going to kick that al'gator under my bed. You watch me." And she crawled under and proceeded to lash out in every direction with her new shoes. "Kick, kick, kick. Dere al'gator. You go 'way." She emerged with a big grin. "He ran 'way. All gone now."

Later, I taught her how to pop dinosaurs, a skill that she has to be reminded of. Then she pops away with glee until they are all gone. Removing her fear of thunder, though, is more challenging. I have not yet come up with a way for her to fight it off.

A few yards further on we find a huge blueberry bush, and Maggie's eyes open wide with delight. "You will give me b'ueberry, please." I strip off half a dozen and put them in her hand, which she claps to her mouth. Delighted, she grabs for more and begins stuffing herself. Then she notices her hands. Her fingers are the color of ink. A horror-stricken look comes over her face. If she could see *that*, I know she would begin wailing. Her lips and chin are solid purple. "Look," she cries out. "Look, I all dirty." And then the inevitable. "Napkin, please. I need napkin."

I explain to her that when people pick blueberries, they expect to get the juice all over their hands. She stares at her blemished fingers uncertainly, then at me. I show her my fingers. Finally, she gives me a nod and grins. "Okay, I wash later," and resumes stuffing her mouth while I fill both our containers.

On the way back to the house, her hands filled with squashed berries and her face awash in blueberry juice, she chortles, "Dat was fun, Daddy. Let's not tell Mat'ew that we went picking b'ueberries, okay?"

August 27

Sometime last night the wind blew up. This morning it is howling and sending great drifts of spray off the bay to slam against the side of the house. Of greater novelty than the wind's force is that it has knocked out the electricity— probably by felling a tree across the wires somewhere, not an infrequent occurrence here. My heart always jumps with excitement when this happens. It isolates us from the rest of the world even more effectively than we already are. The joyous thought crosses my mind that we will have to cook our meals in the fireplace and go to bed this evening by candlelight. Willa is already happily digging in drawers for candles.

The kids, particularly Matthew, are not so happy. A gust of wind has toppled the structure of his little world. When the electricity went off, he was making a banana milk shake in a blender by pushing every button on the appliance. The machine stopped and all the lights went out at once as if an invisible hand had flicked a switch. Matthew looked up confused. When we told him that a tree had probably fallen across the lines, worry clouded his face. "But, Daddy," he yelped. "We won't be able to read books; we won't be able to watch *Sesame Street.* You won't be able to use your typewriter." Maggie caught Matthew's concern like a case of chicken pox, her face furrowing in worry. "No Sesame, Daddy. We can't see Oscar, no Grover. What we going to do?"

That the kids get so upset by nature's mischief reminds me once more that New York, for all the stimulation it offers, does not encourage a give-and-take with the elements, which is why New Yorkers become so distraught over an inch of snow. I would rather that they learn to accept the weather's vagaries like New Englanders.

I decide it would be good for them to see more of the storm's excitement. "Hey," I exclaim, "let's drive around the Point and see if we can see how many trees have fallen down." Matthew looks at me worriedly. "Come on, it's fun to go out in a storm," I tell him in a persuasive voice while I put on a sou'wester.

"Come on, kids. Let's go and see a real storm," Willa adds excitedly. Now that they know that both parents want to see the damage, the feel obligated to muster up some enthusiasm.

"We go see trees crash," Maggie says halfheartedly, then worriedly asks, "Trees get hurt when they fall?"

The road is littered with pine needles and small branches. As the wheels hit puddles, great flumes of spray arc into the underbrush. The dramatic effect begins to light the children's eyes. But the most exciting scene is at the causeway that crosses the marsh. The road is completely flooded, buried under four feet of white-capped water, making the Point an island, its residents cut off. Delighted huddles of people mill about the road where it enters the water. As during any event beyond human control, protective guards are cast aside and conversations flow unfettered. The might of hurricanes and the human heroics acted out during them are the mainstay of the talk. The older generation settles on the 1938 hurricane, the younger one on Hurricane Carol in 1953.

Carol was one of the highlights of my childhood, a hurricane full of suspense and thrills. The day before it struck, my father and I went sailing. The wind was steady, but the air had a breathtaking calmness, as if everything around us hovered at the edge of a gigantic vacuum that would soon suck us into its grasp. Seabirds behaved strangely, flying low over the water in silent lines, gathering in coves that they do not ordinarily frequent. In the harbor, people were hauling rowboats out of the water, reinforcing their sailboats' moorings and talking in tense, quiet tones about when "it" would hit. I didn't know what "it" was, other than a strong wind, but I kept looking toward the open ocean, where I was told the wind would begin to rise.

Early the next morning I awakened in my grandmother's house to a hissing sound. The hurricane was arriving, driving up the bay with an intensity that caused a hiss rather than a groan when it struck the house. While we were still able to, my cousins and I ran outside the house to test the wind's growing force. When we faced it, we were almost bowled over backward unless we lay on the grass and gradually rose so that our bodies were almost parallel to the ground and then launched ourselves forward as if we were trying to crash through a breaking wave on a beach. When we had struggled to the edge of the lawn, we flung ourselves around, raised our arms, and let the wind carry us back again, feeling that this was the closest any of us had ever come to flying and wondering if at any second we would soar into the darkening sky.

The fury grew, clouds swirled in grotesque formations, pine trunks snapped, and the electricity died. The family mounted to the third floor to witness the destruction from a height. White froth covered the bay; spray and rain filled the air. At times, great layers of water lifted right off the ocean. We could see them flying toward us, and when they struck the roof, the entire house would shudder. Waves, made shapeless by the wind, hurtled onto the bluffs and ate away at the soil until great sections of ground caved into the rolling water below, making it a chocolate color.

My grandmother paced back and forth, turning from one member of the family to another, wondering if the house would hold together. The possibility of the roof being ripped off was beyond my comprehension. I was swept up by what was happening outside the windows. The wind's force pushed me into an exhilaration I had never felt before. For me, its dominating power made everyone in the family, everyone in the world, an equal. My childhood fears died, replaced by a surge of happiness.

My father and most of the men in the family were down in the harbor trying to stop wild boats that had broken their moorings from crashing into rocks or other craft. During the storm's eye, when the wind suddenly abated and the sky lightened as if the sun were about to break through, we children were escorted there over fallen trees and snaking telephone and electricity lines so that we could see the damage. My eyes widened. Boats lay broken everywhere along the shore. A yawl had run up on the front lawn of a nearby house. Two men had been aboard. My father said that they had closed themselves into the cabin. When the boat came to rest, my father and some others had forced open the hatch, and there were the two men, tied together in a bunk, both in shock and shaking uncontrollably.

The eye passed quickly, and the winds rose again. The boats that remained at their moorings gave up. One moment they were bobbing up and down, their bows facing the gale, the next they had turned tail as if they did not have the strength to continue battling. Each time, my father ran along the shore to where a boat was about to run aground to try to coax it to a gentle resting place. He was a distant hero to me then. I loved to see him grab a line and with other rescuers heave a boat onto the sand. The storm had changed him, too. It had channeled his energy from striking out in rage to making desperate rescue attempts. I felt close to him for the good the hurricane had done to us; it had swept away my fear of him and his need to criticize me. In my gratitude, I wanted the wind to scream forever.

Matthew stands listening to the stories of his elders. He makes sporadic wading forays along the inundated road. His eyes sparkle and he holds out his arms to feel the wind push back his palms. On the return to the house he says, "I hope the electricity has not come back on. We can build a fire and camp in the house. Storms are fun. They make people talk a lot." I agree.

August 28

The water remains rolled in the wake of the storm, the wind still brisk. There will be no swimming, sailing, or fishing today. The tennis court is soaked, the rocks along the shore slippery, and the secret paths soggy. At half-low tide this afternoon, Matthew and I go to the tidal pool to dig for cherrystones. Residents of the Point love the tidal pool for its eternal peace as well as for what it holds, hundreds upon hundreds of quahogs. There is an unwritten rule that allows them to indulge two or three times a summer in a few dozen of its cherrystones. The informality of the spirit of conservation here runs strong. A person could probably extinguish the pond's clam population in a few days of digging. Someone did his best a few years ago, but he was not a resident. He was a professional clam digger and he came with his boat and sacks on high tide, poling right up the tidal creek without trespassing for a second on private land. The man began digging and dug through the day while the residents stood on the shore and watched the moral violation, helpless to do anything about it. The clam digger was within his legal rights.

They could have thrown stones at him, but they did not. They could have yelled at him. They did not. They just stared at him. They gathered in groups by the edge of the pool and stared. By the middle of the afternoon, the man began glancing up uneasily and twisting his neck around to see if anyone was sneaking up behind him. Suddenly, he heaved a half-filled sack in his boat, jumped in, and disappeared down the tidal creek. Bushels of clams remained in the mud, but he never returned.

We have enjoyed only a brief taste of cherrystones from the pool this summer. Time is running out and we want a second taste. Matthew is the only child I know who loves raw clams. He approaches a plate of cherrystones on the half shell with ecstasy on his face. His eyes roam over the morsels before he methodically begins picking up each shell and slurping the contents into his mouth. Oysters receive the same attention.

The tidal pool holds mystery as well as clams. It is easiest to enter it via the creek where the water is shallow and swift running. As one approaches the still water of the pool, minnows by the thousands flutter in tight schools out of the path of churning feet. Little spider crabs, their shells camouflaged by a coating of algae, lazily walk away on long legs. An occasional eel undulates in the weak current. The shells of a dozen species of clam litter the floor, which turns increasingly muddier and softer. Where the living relatives of these clams dwell is a mystery to me, for I have never found any other clam species here but quahogs. But then, for all the years that I have waded about the tidal pool, I have never explored its far side against the tall pines. I am scared to; it looks too primitive over there, the water forever unruffled. It's too quiet, the water, or the mud beneath it, too ready to grab an intruder.

Besides, I have long imagined that the descendants of the crabs netted by that nanny dwell in safety on the far side of the pond, waiting for an opportunity to take their revenge.

Matthew knows nothing about these fears, however. His only concern is the underwater jungles of silt-laden algae and plants clinging to the near side of the pool's bottom. They are so thick that the mud between the clumps looks like oases of safety. There is no telling what is hiding in that soft vegetation. Matthew is nervous and cries out when he sees small crabs scurrying for its protection. I, too, feel some qualms but plunge my feet downward in a show of fearlessness. Matthew follows by jumping carefully from my footprint to footprint, enjoying, I think, the feel of the mud oozing between his toes. When I reach a large barren section of mud, I squat down and burrow my fingers through it until I feel the shape of a clam. The bottom of our wire basket is quickly covered with them.

Matthew's interest in the hunt becomes only peripheral as his fascination with the mud's texture deepens. Soon he becomes a happy hog in a wallow, lying down in the shallow water and throwing mud over his back. The water thickens with particles of slime, takes on the color of sewage, and lets off an odor both repulsive and fascinating for the eons of life and death it represents. All of him disappears except for his head. Then he tells me that he is going to duck his head under. I cry out in alarm, scared that he will forever disappear in the decay. A sensation of jealousy also flits through my mind; his abandon in the mud has taken on a fervor of happiness. He throws clumps of it about; he belly flops into its stench; he smears it over his body in a rite of worship that I never experienced as a child here. Matthew and the mud that is the source of so much of Weenaumet Point have become one.

August 29

The east wind pushes *Song Sparrow* smartly out of the harbor and down the channel toward the bay. As usual, Matthew prances about the cockpit and jumps up onto the bow. Maggie, all but hidden by her life preserver, is content to remain seated astern. When we round the island's point and have to tack several times to reach its sweeping beach, she shouts, "I stay here," an incongruous response to my "Ready about, hardalee." The island looks deserted as we approach it, low lying and scruffy, dotted with clumps of cedars surrounded by high-strutting poison ivy. The marsh grass, metallic in the sun and somber green in the shade, provides the only softness to the view.

In a flurry, we heave the anchor and drop the mainsails. Matthew has become very involved in boats. He wants to do everything—raise, lower, and furl sails; pump the bilge; haul and let out sheets. We encourage and help him. But there are some things he cannot do, such as throw the heavy anchor overboard. He whimpers because I would not let him do this, and I make up a story to distract him as I row us ashore in *Turkey,* our dilapidated rowboat, christened by Matthew.

It's another pirate-treasure story. These have become

a staple. I feel badly that for all the stories I have made up about pirates, we have not found any exciting treasure on our hunts, not even a lost fishing lure. "Matthew," I begin in a serious way, "this is a mostly deserted island. No one ever comes here, but a long time ago in the olden days, pirates came here to bury their treasure. If we look hard, we might find some of it." Matthew's face has grown solemn at my mention of pirates but brightens when he hears "treasure." Maggie is oblivious, sitting in Willa's lap pointing at seagulls. "See birdie, dat's gullbirdie."

This may be the last chance we have to sail and explore this summer. In the bow of *Turkey,* Matthew scans the island's shore. It looks especially forlorn today, though the sun shines and the sky is a deep blue. Green seaweed lies limp on the rocks exposed by low tide. But high tides have lined the beach with brown furrows of wet eelgrass. The east wind ruffles the dune grass in a direction it is not accustomed to, showing us its dull underside.

When the boat grinds upon the pebbles, Matthew steps out hesitantly, but I can see excitement boiling in his eyes. Of all the places we have looked for pirate treasure, this offers the greatest possibilities. The island's spine is made of soft sand where treasure chests could easily be buried. He points to two wind-lashed cedars. "Let's go over there," he suggests with a sort of Huckleberry Finn logic. "Pirates might have liked to bury their treasure under trees so they would know where to find it when they came back." The trees are up a small sandy rise that is set back from the beach. We start along a path that seems to lead in that direction. When it opens onto a sandy area empty of grass, Matthew suddenly gasps and kneels down. "Look, a pirate button!"

There glistening in the sand is a flat piece of rounded shell with two holes through its center. A few paces further on, he again exclaims and points toward the sand at his feet. "Old metal," he yells. "Maybe it was a pirate chest that got too old." The ground is specked with fragments of rust. We begin to dig furiously with our hands and with pieces of shell. Matthew's excitement is contagious. I keep thinking how I would feel if we uncovered the corner of a chest. But no. Just sand and more sand. Matthew's pace slows, and I see disappointment soften his face.

I have to do something to extricate both of us from this dilemma. So I lie again and distract Matthew by telling him I thought I just saw a whale spout out in the bay. When he is looking hard out to the water, I dig down into my pocket and come up with a handful of change, which I throw in the hole and cover with a layer of sand.

"Well, Matthew, let's dig a little more," I say, trying to put disappointment in my voice. He turns back with his shell. A nickel shows up, then a penny, then a quarter. He smiles and grabs them. But his smile tells me he knows damn well where they came from. I feel foolish.

"Dad, put them back in the hole. Let's find them again."

I do so while Matthew looks elsewhere, pretending not to know what I am doing. Then he digs again and retrieves the coin.

"Look, Dad. Pirates really were here."

August 30

Matthew came into our room long before dawn to announce that he had to go "do," still an event for a four-and-a-half-year-old, demanding parental reaction. I mumbled my approval and he asked me to come with him to the bathroom. Eyes still tight with sleep, he slumped on the toilet and did his "do." Then he asked me to wipe him, a parent's duty that is not as unpleasant as one might imagine. Matthew has been making great strides toward independent toileting, prompted by my telling him that in kindergarten, which he will begin in a few weeks, children are expected to go unattended.

He liked the idea and applied himself to the task with diligence. But last night, sleep and darkness caused a regression, though the desire for independence was there. Conflict resulted. At 3:00 A.M. tension hovered about the toilet and erupted as I leaned over to wipe him. In a dream state, he snarled at me and grabbed at the paper. I shrank back as if a dog had lunged at me. It was not the mere mood swing of a little boy; it was adult anger.

I returned to bed disturbed by the knowledge that I had just witnessed the workings of a human time warp, the kind of anger that Matthew might display fifteen years from now. When I was old enough to muster this kind of anger against my father, he backed away just as I had done. It helped us to understand each other, at least to the extent that we could better communicate, albeit silently.

When I was sixteen, I hurled a glass of his whiskey across the room. My parents were in the habit of having a few drinks every evening before dinner. We often sat together struggling for harmony at these times. Once, I had just written a front-page story for my school newspaper. My father picked it up and began questioning me about some of the words I had chosen. His tone was belligerent. Had he criticized me for almost anything else, I would have silently listened and grown a little bit sadder. But writing was becoming too precious. He knew nothing about words and had little curiosity about them. His reading consisted of the daily newspaper and magazines and books about sailing. Yet he had just attacked a newly discovered fabric that I was learning to weave into a net that would both save me from falling into despair and provide me with the one means of communication in which my fear of ridicule would be overcome. If he destroyed this, there would be nothing left.

I attacked the glass of bourbon because it was liquor that encouraged particularly harsh words to tumble from my father's mouth. When I picked it up, the words stopped. The sudden stillness was lovely as the glass sailed through the air. It smashed against the wall with an echoing ring; the pieces tinkled to the floor, and the liquid streaked the wallpaper with delicate designs. My father turned on me and barked something to the effect of "Why did you do that?" But I heard a hollowness in the words. I looked at him and saw fear flicker over his eyes.

That was not the last of our confrontations. The last

one was on Weenaumet Point early one winter after a snowfall. By that time, my father had suffered three heart attacks and two strokes. He had recovered from each one, though they had diminished his outward fire. I was shoveling snow, and the blade caught on the edge of a wooden step and splintered it. Just as writing was my net, the house was my father's. He heard the sound and saw that I had damaged the one thing in his life that he felt proud of. Once again, he yelled at me. He ridiculously accused me of intentionally destroying his house. I realized then the extent of the fear with which he regarded me, the possibility that his son might sweep him off his feet by chipping away at his only crutch. For years, my mother had told me how jealous he had grown of me. Here was the proof.

"I am not destroying your house," I screamed at him. "You're scared that I will destroy you."

He looked baffled; my father was a man of little psychological insight. "I saw what you did to those steps," he snapped. But his eyes flitted from mine as he said it.

I felt sad then. "You're not angry at me about the steps; just a splinter of wood came off. You're mad at me because I have gone far beyond your image of me. You're mad because I am young and I am going away. You're mad because you have lived in fear all your life and never been able to admit it to anyone."

His face turned white. He clutched the back of a chair, and I thought that he was going to have another heart attack. He stared at me with tearful eyes. "Yes," he murmured. "And now I am scared of dying." That was the most honest and revealing thing he ever said to me.

Two weeks later, a large package was delivered to my apartment in New York. I was preparing to set off for Louisiana to begin research on my first book, the one about the Mississippi River delta. The package contained a much-needed electric typewriter. There was no message. I knew it was a terribly silent effort by my father to help me in my writing. It was also an acknowledgment of my escape.

Three weeks later, he was dead.

August 31

The last full day. The children are strangely silent as we clean up. They sense change. Matthew is in his plastic wading pool, in which he sails a gaff-rigged model sailboat not too unlike *Song Sparrow*. His passengers are figures of Darth Vader, Luke Skywalker, R2D2, and a few innocent-looking children with no legs, lifted from Maggie's box of toys. He is sailing them around the pool, telling them about the coast of Africa, pirate treasure, and the last dinosaur.

Maggie runs back and forth across the width of the deck, flapping her arms and trying to keep up with the gulls that effortlessly drift by. They eye her curiously. As each disappears, leaving Maggie grounded, she waves and quietly tells them, "Bye-bye, gull. See you later."

A month in the house has turned its shipshape orderliness to chaos. Cleaning is an all-day ordeal. In the process we come upon articles of the kids' clothing that have been missing for days. I also discover something that startles me.

The basement is full of paraphernalia accumulated by my father. He never threw anything away. After he died, we came upon bank statements going back fifty years. Hooks and nails are draped with lengths of rope and electrical wiring that he collected. The space between the ceiling joists and house beams holds caches of lead fishing weights, golf balls, and boxes of shackles. Timbers of various dimensions and heights lean against the walls. Many have fallen or are askew, making the place look like the periphery of a lumberyard. I decide to straighten them up, not throw them out, for, like my father, I have found that such odds and ends are always useful, though they may rest untouched for years.

Matthew hears me crashing around and comes to investigate with a cheerful "I thought there was a monster in the basement making all that noise. Dad, are you a monster?" Then he begins to help me. In one corner, a pile of six-by-twelves leans crookedly against the wall. Sawed-off beam ends left over from the construction of the house, they have been there since it was finished sixteen years ago. They could stay there in disarray, but I am offended by their messy appearance, so I tell Matthew that our last job is to arrange the timbers so that they stand upright against the wall. Matthew runs to the task and begins heaving one of the beams upright. He can scarcely lift it but soon angles it upright away from its resting place. Then he calls to me. "Look, Dad, there's writing on the wall. What does it say?"

What is written on the concrete in barely distinguishable pencil is HOUSE FINISHED and underneath, AUGUST 1969. The writing is in my father's hand.

What made him commemorate the completion of the house by scrawling these words and numbers on the wall, I will never know. At least, I suppose that is what they signify. He certainly chose a humble means and untrafficked place. Then it struck me. He probably never wanted anyone to see the writing; he wrote it for himself, a private reminder that here was something at last that he had accomplished. In moments of unhappiness as the years went by, he may have come down here, pried away the beams, and gazed upon this crude little inscription.

September 1

A pungent crispness flavors the crystal air, making you want to stop and just breathe. The water is limpid and dances along the shore. The kids react to our leaving much more naturally than I. They yell; they scream and whine; they kick and pull each other's hair. Matthew is in his underwear and refuses to dress himself further. Maggie throws Cheerios on the floor.

My uncle pops in the door to say good-bye and cannot help but remark on the children's behavior. "Well, I guess the place has really gotten to them," he says happily.

At last everything is in order and the car packed. I am just about to give the door a final slam shut when Matthew sneaks past me and into the house. I say nothing. The look on his face has a determination to it. He goes up to the fireplace mantel and stares for a moment at the photograph of my father sailing and then he says, "Good-bye, Grandpa Bill, we had a nice summer."

Author's Note

Weenaumet Point cannot be found on a map. It does exist somewhere on Buzzards Bay, though with a different name. I have chosen not to reveal the Point's real name or exact location out of deference to those who live there, people whose high regard for privacy has been honed over generations. Weenaumet Point is changing fast enough not to have its transformation exacerbated by those who are merely curious to see its beauty or try to catch a glimpse of its elusive personality.